ISBN: 143823581X

This book is dedicated to my loving wife, Christine.

Contents

Bonus Content

CHAPTER 1

In The Beginning......

I was born the day after Christmas 1969. Growing up in the suburbs of Baltimore I enjoyed a standard middle class life. Public schools, little league baseball and vacations at the beach were routine in our neighborhood. Both of my parents worked hard to give my sister and me a better life than they had. We weren't wealthy. My first car was an ugly 1979 Maverick that cost $600. My second was a 1979 Nova complete with gold paint and the most hideous cloth checkered seats ever made. We were a typical middle class family for our area.

As an adolescent I didn't necessarily enjoy school, but I didn't despise it either. I got A's and B's without much effort. It wasn't until 7th grade that I began hiding my report cards from my parents. Also around this time, my desire to play baseball and basically be a good kid waned. My teenage years were full of angst, energy and great times. I was popular, sat at the 'cool' lunch table & mostly cruised my way through high school. I remember sitting before the vice-principal the second week of my senior year discussing my attendance problem. Summers were spent bouncing around at the beach, holding down a menial paying job and partying.

"If you don't go to college, David, you'll end up a ditch digger.....", was all I ever heard from my mother since I was born. Things like success or a career were never discussed in our house unless college was part of the game plan. My parents were both part of the 1940's baby boom generation: grow up, get married, settle down, get a good 9 to 5 job with benefits and stay there until retirement. They watched as others with college diplomas leapt up the corporate ladder so I can understand their belief that a degree equaled advancement. Unfortunately, for them, college or any other type of continuing education was never on my mind.

From my early teens through my early twenties I went through what I can only describe as my 'floundering period'. I didn't know exactly what I wanted to do or where I wanted to go, but I knew I was destined for something. I'm not talking about having my face on the big screen or becoming President; it was a yearning to be above average. The last thing I envisioned was working a 'safe' 9 to 5 job handcuffed to a cubicle as a another cog in the workforce machine. It was around this time that I knew I would never be truly happy unless I was my own boss, answering to no one, and master of how I spent my time.

"The most delightful surprise in life is to suddenly recognize your own worth"
-Maxwell Maltz

This is important. If you don't already have a feeling in your gut, in your soul, that you are far greater than your current circumstances, you need to start envisioning yourself as a leader & decision maker now. More on this later.

Things take a turn for the better, and worse.

In 1993 at the age of 23, I started dating my future wife Christine. I honestly don't know what she saw in me at that time. It must be true that behind every great man is a great woman. I think at the core she saw in me solid character and 'potential'. She had recently completed 6 years at Loyola College with a Masters Degree in speech pathology and was making good money. Her upbringing consisted of private schools, country clubs outside of Washington DC, condo at the beach, etc.

I, at the time, was working at a liquor store and living with my parents. What a catch, huh? I had an eleven year old car that belched smoke, no money and even worse- no prospects. I had nothing on the horizon and certainly no set plan. So what did we do? That's right, we moved in together. I sold a few items in the Pennysaver to come up with my share of the deposit ($300) and away we went. It was a tiny 2 bedroom apartment with no central air conditioning and a kitchen the size of a walk in closet. It's funny to think back on that experience now. Our first night there we watched the movie Grease, ate pizza and slept on the floor. To quote the old saying, "We were poor, but we were happy".

It was around this time that television infomercials were on the rise. I had seen the Anthony Robbins infomercials for years and even though they always intrigued me, I had never purchased his material. For whatever reason, that year I took the plunge and ordered his '30 Day Program for Unlimited Success'. Like many, my life did not transform in thirty days to the life of my dreams. On the contrary, everything seemed to keep sliding downhill.

My job at the liquor store had come to a mutual end, so I turned my sights onto building a bigger & better life. Adapting to the Tony Robbins program, I started to set physical, financial and personal goals for myself. For the next year I basically sponged money from my parents while writing the next 'Great American Novel'. It was a fictional tale of two brothers, a funeral home and a crazy storyline. After distributing the manuscript to several publishers and receiving a stack of non-personal rejection letters, I decided to start a direct mail business that sold information on personal development. Using cash advances on three credit cards, I created slick brochures and purchased mailing addresses from direct mail companies. I had a semi-professional picture taken in my only suit so that anyone receiving my direct mail piece would see me as 'legitimate'.

If someone had been videotaping me at the time, how pathetic I must have looked going downstairs everyday to our dingy apartment mailbox to check for orders. To this day I can recognize the sound of a postal truck engine.

It didn't take long for this shortsighted idea (and my monthly bills) to max out my credit cards. On June 10, 1995 Christine & I married and traveled to Barbados for our honeymoon. We used a small bank loan, wedding gift cash and a family member in the travel business to swing the all-inclusive trip. Unfortunately, I couldn't allow myself to fully enjoy the Caribbean splendor that surrounded us. I didn't think I deserved to enjoy it while financial storm clouds loomed at home.

By the end of June I was dodging creditors phone calls and scrambling to stay afloat. I visited a credit counseling service and a very polite gentleman told me there was nothing they could do. I had no income and therefore no strategy for repaying my debts. He did say that he could offer some advice. When I asked him to explain, he said that company policy would not permit it to be discussed. For a few seconds I was extremely confused and then it hit me- he was advising me to claim bankruptcy.

This was one of those watershed moments when you start thinking that maybe your parents were right. Maybe I should've gone to college. Maybe the reason the majority of people drudgingly accept mediocre jobs is so they won't end up in my situation. Maybe that's why I was pawning a guitar and a handful of CD's, just so I could buy groceries, while the great majority were at their jobs.

In July of 1995 I was twenty six years old, newly married, living in a tiny apartment with no steady job and bankrupt. I had filed for Chapter 7 bankruptcy protection for just under 30k in debt. Having the weight of the world on your shoulders was no longer an abstract saying to me. I felt as though I could do nothing right.

Desperate for money, I took a job delivering the paper during the day and delivering pizza at night. I can't even put into words the embarrassment I felt every single day. One of Christine's old college roommates lived in our apartment complex and a neighbor of hers was a customer on my morning route. I used to sneak along the side of the building, toss the paper inside quickly and scamper away with my tail between my legs. My dignity was at an all time low.

I decided to take a job with Coca-Cola that involved re-stocking shelves in the large grocery store chains. Part of the job was to create large displays that sit at the end of an aisle when their product is on sale. After stocking 6 to 10 stores a day while wearing heavy steel-toe boots, I would come back to our little apartment and not move. Everything from the back of my neck to the bottom of my feet ached every night. It was hard manual labor and I knew I couldn't keep it up for very long. Even worse than how it affected me physically was how emotionally & mentally drained I was becoming. I knew I was capable of so much more and it crushed me that I had accomplished so little with my life.

After several months I got a job selling computer software for a small local company. Christine was happy that I finally had a salaried position with health benefits and a Monday to Friday work schedule. I was thrilled to no longer come home aching and tired every night. Maybe now I could finally tap into some of that unused potential inside of me.

It was the end of 1995 and I was making $15,000 a year plus commission.

CHAPTER 2

"Forget past mistakes. Forget failures. Forget everything except what you're going to do now and do it."
-William Durant

When most of us hear of someone hitting rock bottom we tend to think of drugs & alcohol consuming their lives. Financially, I was at my bottom. Even worse, I was devastated emotionally. I give a lot of credit to Tony Robbins at this point in my life. He talks about hitting bottom, hitting a threshold where you tell yourself- ENOUGH! I am greater than my current circumstances and I refuse to live like this anymore.

Anyone who has ever reached this point knows what I mean. I'm not talking about self-pity or just mere words. It's in your gut. It's like a hot flash burning inside you trying to get out. I felt a massive urge to do something, to create something, to take some sort of action. I started thinking about my wife & how much she wanted to start a family. Having a professional career was not something she dreamed about as a child. She wanted to be a stay-at-home mom with a two car garage house and white picket fence.

The thought of her having to go to a job instead of raising our children hurt me deeply. The idea of our kids going to day care instead of being raised at home with their mom caused me an incredible amount of pain. Not having the house we wanted, not being able to go on vacation, living with a feeling of 'lack', were all devastating possibilities that I wanted to avoid at any cost. I was willing to do whatever it took, with exception of theft or anything else that violated my character & principles, to be successful.

It's indescribable how much motivation these feelings gave me. This is when I began to reach deep inside myself and focus like a laser on creating the life I wanted. I started to ask myself one question, "How can I replace my wife's income without having to work two jobs?" This one simple, yet powerful, question pulled me in a direction that would forever change my life. I was about to take the first steps towards 'designing a life' instead of 'just getting by'. It's the difference between getting up before sunrise because you have to be at work by 8:00am, and getting up before sunrise even though you could stay in bed all day if you wished.

One of my main reasons for writing this book is to hopefully open your eyes to this difference. It's a mindset and once it's turned on, there's really no way to turn it off. It's the difference between looking forward to your lunch break & eventually the drive home, and looking forward to being the master of your day.

"When your desires are strong enough, you
will possess superhuman powers to achieve".
-Napoleon Hill

The Library. What a quaint concept.

I don't know why I thought this was a good place to start, but it seemed logical to go to the library for information. Maybe it was because I was broke & couldn't afford to buy a book. Not knowing where to start or even exactly what I was looking for, I located the library catalog and typed in the word 'money'. I wrote down a few of the shelf numbers then typed in 'wealth'. I noticed that the numbers were very close together and sure enough a quick walk down that aisle had my heart pumping. I had just struck gold.

In this section of the library were all the titles that related not only to money or wealth, but also the stock market, accounting, multi-level marketing, biographies of the rich, franchises, real estate & day trading. I randomly picked enough books to fill a paper bag and went back to the apartment with my booty.

I spent the next several weeks pouring over book after book. To be honest, many of them were lousy. As I read of all the various ways to create income, it didn't take long to see that real estate was my best bet. Buying a franchise seemed no different than 'buying' yourself a full-time job. Lots of money has been made in the stock market, but you realistically need a chunk of money & a clear understanding of how the market worked. A stock position could change at any moment, while you're busy at your job, and suddenly your little nest egg is emptied.

Real estate seemed to reach out and grab me. If done creatively it required very little, if any, money. It also had a real entrepreneurial spirit about it. There is one person in those early days whose writing really inspired me and made me believe that I could become wealthy through real estate. His name is Robert Allen.

Robert Allen has been a pioneer in creative real estate investing for decades. His first two books, Creating Wealth and Nothing Down, are must reads for anyone involved in this business. They were originally written in the 80's and may seem a bit dated, but what's most important are the concepts and ideas. The prices & numbers are low by today's standards, but his concepts for buying real estate laid the foundation for my knowledge in this area.

Books are my number one resource. As I began to make money, I graduated from the library to full fledge book ownership. My home office is now filled with books; so many that I have boxes full of books in storage.

I have also purchased tape programs about real estate investment and attended seminars. All of these have value, but be leery of anything costing hundreds of dollars. There may be some good tips in them, but far too many are long on words and short on results. A lot of the seminars are 'free', but after an hour of someone's rah-rah pitch you're hit with the real reason they want you there- they're selling a $500 investment program.

You can lay your foundation of wealth for free by becoming a regular at your local branch library.

To be a Real Estate Licensee or not to be….

If you're serious about investing in real estate and are ready to do whatever it takes to achieve your goals, I recommend that you get a real estate license. Having a working knowledge of creative techniques found in books is great, but in addition you'll need a solid understanding of contract law, title & deed preparation, etc.

When crunch time comes and you're writing offers, you will be measurably more confident as a licensed real estate agent. Imagine negotiating with another agent that's representing a seller of a property you want. They may have twenty years of experience and know the market blindfolded. You, on the other hand, have just read a bunch of books and are now jumping into the market. You'll be much more prepared and make better deals after getting your license.

Real estate is a business. When you sign a contract, it's a binding agreement. Even if you're planning on using a real estate agent to locate properties for you, it's in your best interest to know the details every step of the way.

Let me let you in on a little secret. This is something I heard years ago on a tape program. I don't remember the speaker or what topic he was discussing, but I clearly remember at one point he walked over to a wall and smacked his hand against it a couple of times. He then looked at the attendees and said something you should never forget. It's a mindset that will determine how far you'll really go in this business. He said, "This wall, this whole building, doesn't care who owns it. Real estate investing is not about the property, it's about relationships. It's about people."

Go back and read that last paragraph again. How well you handle your interpersonal relationships will ultimately be the determining factor in your success. Educating yourself in this area will work wonders and I highly recommend that you expand beyond just wanting financial success. Becoming an effective communicator takes time but it is well worth the effort.

For right now, just know that becoming a licensed real estate agent is a worthwhile endeavor. As you add more knowledge to your foundation, the better communicator you will be.

Warning....

First, don't be surprised if you're the only investor in your real estate licensing class. During the real estate market surge of 2000 to 2005, the number of people who became licensed agents skyrocketed. Most of these people were looking to become a typical agent- listing homes, selling homes, attending open houses, etc. Many of them would've skipped the class if they could, their only desire was to have the actual license.

Your goal is knowledge. I was a terrible student in grade school, but in my license class I excelled next to my lackluster classmates. One simple thing I did was use 3x5 cards as a study aid. Between license and contract law, Federal housing laws, lending and title there is an awful lot of terminology. I would write a word on one side of the card and its definition on the other, then have my wife quiz me until I knew them all. I was in my mid-twenties and was the youngest in my class. I remember a woman commenting that it was easier for me because I was younger and had been in a school-type setting more recently than the others. I politely nodded and shrugged it off, but inside I was insulted.

It wasn't luck and it wasn't because I was younger. It was because I was willing to work a little harder that made me succeed in the class.

"Nothing worthwhile comes easily. Half effort does not produce half results. It produces no results. Work, continuous work and hard work, is the only way to accomplish results that last"
-Hamilton Holt

Second, don't get caught up into the competitiveness of a typical real estate office. In Maryland, and in most states, once you have a real estate license you must be associated with a real estate broker. After passing the licensee exam I made an appointment with the manager of a local Long & Foster real estate office.

Between office meetings & 'war stories' from the more seasoned agents, it didn't take long before the competitive nature of the sales force took hold of me. I quickly lost focus of the original reason I got a license- to be a better investor and to have access to the MLS (multiple listing service). Soon I was beating the bushes for listings and spending my weekends at open houses.

Fortunately after a couple of listings & sales and performing like a traditional agent, I re-focused and got back on track as a beginner investor.

There was something interesting that I noticed about most of the agents. The vast majority were accustomed to bread-and-butter transactions, this being homebuyers & homesellers, standard inspection & financing addendums, etc. As soon as you started talking about investment property or creative investing their eyes glazed over. A few might have had an idea of what you're talking about, but most resisted anything that was 'outside the box'.

To this day, after buying & selling millions of dollars worth of real estate I would still be unable to convince some real estate agents that you can buy property with no money down & have a positive cash flow and walk away from settlement with a cashier's check that's tax free.

I know it's possible. I've done it numerous times. Financial prosperity surrounds us in this country and yet most people walk around with a feeling of lack. They believe they lack opportunities, lack the right connections or that they're not smart enough. These are all just excuses and most people have thousands of them.

Whether you believe you can accomplish something or believe you can't- you're right!

I choose to believe I can and that has made all the difference.

"Both optimists and pessimists contribute to society. The optimist invents the airplane, the pessimist the parachute".
-George Bernard Shaw

CHAPTER 3

My first deal. The Kitchen Table Offer….

My wife was not thrilled with the idea of still living in our tiny apartment after we got married. I was feeling the pressure so I began scanning the Baltimore Sun real estate section for a house. Since we were operating on extremely limited money I narrowed my focus to ads that emphasized some sort of help with the closing costs.

I called several ads trying to find the right seller with flexibility and motivation. I found a 3 bedroom, 2 full & 2 half-bathroom townhouse in the suburbs of the city. The area seemed pretty good with a nice mall and lots of newer stores within minutes of the house.

Turning off of the main road and into the neighborhood the houses looked rather bland. Not ugly, but not terribly exciting either. Our future home was no different. It had off white vinyl siding, a covered front porch and a front yard not much bigger than a postage stamp. There was an odd thatch of strawberry plants lining both sides of the sidewalk leading up to the front door.

We sat in the car and debated whether or not it was even worth looking at the inside. Since it took us twenty minutes to get there, it made sense to at least give the interior a quick look.

The first floor had a living room, powder room and a huge kitchen that blew us away. We were used to our apartment galley kitchen that allowed for no more than 2 people at a time. This one measured 12x17 with an island and a sliding glass door to the backyard. Upstairs was another treat. The master bedroom had a nice walk-in closet and the master bath boasted a double sink. The basement was finished and included a fireplace, wet bar and another bathroom.

Don't misunderstand, this place was not a palace. But compared to the 500 sqft. apartment we'd been occupying for the last three years, this house felt massive. I reminded Christine to keep her composure & let me do the talking as we left the basement to speak to the owner.

After some friendly prodding I discovered that the owner's had moved to another county to care of a sick relative (motivation) and since they had bought the house just 5 years ago using a VA loan, they were happy to just break even and get rid of the house (flexibility).

I told them that we could give them their asking price of $113,000 but I said that we had limited money and that they would have to contribute substantially to our closing costs. They agreed and with that I went to the car and grabbed a contract. I sat at their kitchen table and quickly wrote my first deal. Two months later and exactly five months from the day of our wedding, we bought the house on November 10,1995. We used $2,000 in gift money from our wedding, $880 in savings and used a cash advance on a credit card for $1,000 to come up with the money to close.

I was delighted to get us out of the apartment and Christine couldn't have been happier. Because of my bad credit and checkered work history, only Christine qualified for the loan and only her name was on the deed to the house. But I really didn't care. What mattered was that the goal of getting out of the apartment had been achieved. If I had let my ego get in the way and waited until both of us could qualify, who knows? We might still be in that damn cramped apartment.

"I know the price of success: dedication, hard work and an unremitting devotion to the things you want to see happen"
-Frank Lloyd Wright

What if the toilet breaks….

By early1996 I was married, living in our townhouse, idling in a $15,000 a year job and hunting for my first investment property deal. One day while looking at another property, I came across a vacant house with a notice on the front window. It was a government foreclosure with a standard notice on it stating that the property had been winterized and included a contact number in case of emergency.

After calling the number, I discovered that this house was a Community Development Association (CDA) foreclosure. In Maryland, the CDA issues a bond on a regular basis totaling over a million dollars. The money raised is then used to provide low interest loans to applicants who can't qualify under other programs. After a foreclosure the property is re-sold through the Maryland Housing Fund. At the time they had an inventory of about fifty houses in Baltimore city. I promptly had my name added to their monthly mailing list for all of their properties for sale.

It didn't take long to come across a decent prospect. Located fifty feet from a large park, 13 N. Linwood Street would practically become my second home for the next couple of months. After a little negotiating with the MD Housing Fund, I was able to buy the house for $31,900. To make it easier I again put the house in my wife's name and we got a FHA 203(k) rehab loan. This loan program has gone through numerous evolutions since 1996, but the basic parameters remain the same.

Basically, I was able to borrow the money for the purchase and have money for the repairs set aside until the house was fixed up. After improvements I received a check for the repair money escrow. One smart thing I did was overestimate my repair costs. I knew that I was going to be doing most of the work on the house myself, so the cost of labor was going to be just my time. With the purchase price of $31,900, I estimated the repairs at $8,750 for the loan. The repairs would actually cost me about $3,000. So at settlement I borrowed $5,000 off of a credit card, bought the house, did the repairs, received the repair escrow check for $8,750, paid off the credit card and rented the house. It rented for $675 a month and the tenant paid all the utilities including water. My total monthly payment including property taxes & insurance (PITI) was $390 giving me a monthly cash flow of $285 less any maintenance. I quickly saw that if I had 10 or 20 or 50 of these houses that some of my dreams would be realized.

I know that what I just described sounds pretty good. I found a house, fixed it up, got it rented and it seemed so easy. Right?

Let me be the first to break this to you: Like many endeavors real estate investing is simple, but it is far from easy. Unlike most business & real estate books, tapes, seminars, etc. that leave off the details, I want to give you a glimpse of what I experienced after buying the house.

For starters, it took me weeks to get the utilities turned on because I kept missing the Baltimore Gas & Electric employee. I sat in my car for hours waiting for them to show up (Quick Hint- use combo lockboxes on your properties & freely give out the combination to contractors, utility workers, etc. Your time is too valuable to be wasted by someone else's schedule). Then once I had everything turned on, I left to go to the store and came back to a flood. A cracked radiator on the 2nd floor caused a small waterfall down the steps and the water then pooled all over the main floor of the house.

Before going to settlement, during the repairs & even after it was rented I was constantly reminded of everything that could go wrong with this venture. I know that most of my friends & family had the best of intentions because they probably didn't want to see me fail. The question is: How do I know if I'm going to succeed, or fail, if I've never done this before? The list was endless: What if nobody rents it? What if the toilet leaks? What if the heat turns off in the middle of the night? How will I find a tenant? How will I keep track of rents &

expenses? What if the tenant stops paying rent? I'm not exaggerating, the list of excuses not to do this was endless.

I had one firm answer then and I use it often to this day. If I come across a situation that I haven't dealt with before my immediate response is- 'I don't know, but I'll figure it out'. I'll do whatever it takes and I'll get it done. If the tenant stops paying rent, I'll figure out how to legally evict them (and I did). If the heat goes up at night in the dead of winter, I'll figure out what to do to get the heat working again (that's happened too). Most people stop far too short of their potential because of irrational fears; fears of failure, fears of success, fears of rejection. They let their fears control them, and maybe worse, they project their fears on other people unintentionally.

Let me explain it another way. Let's say you have a rich uncle who just passed away. You weren't very close to him, but in his will he left you a nice 3 unit apartment building located about 20 minutes from where you live. The property is given to you free and clear. There's no mortgage and similar properties in that area are selling for $150,000. Two of the apartments are rented for $700 each and the other unit needs a little work to get it ready to rent again. All the utilities are separated for each apartment except the water.

What would your reaction be to hearing this news? Would you be in a panic about a possible toilet leaking? Would you be nervous about finding a tenant to fill the vacancy? If the heating system needed to be looked at, would that leave you in a cold sweat at night?

I doubt it.

More likely, your mind would be racing with ideas and possibilities. The heat isn't working? No problem. You open the phone book and look under the heading 'Heat'. You spend 15 minutes making calls until you find someone that seems reasonably priced and you get them out there.

What have you just done? You figured it out, took a little action and got it done. The difference is in your mental attitude. Some people allow themselves to be buried in the details and walk in fear every step of the way. The rest of us accept the fact that we don't have an answer for every situation, but we do have the courage & persistence to get things done and resolve any problems as they inevitably arise.

The other thing you should know relating to the purchase of 13 N. Linwood is my level of commitment to getting a project done. At least 4 days during the week I would work from 8:30am to 5:00pm at my computer software sales job, then change into work clothes and drive into the city. I would usually work at the house until 10:00pm then head home. On Saturday & Sunday I would work in the early morning & afternoon and try to be home by 5:00pm. I became a rare sight at many family get-togethers and my wife knew me as a lump in the bed during the week. She didn't complain, though. We both knew this was the hard work & sacrifice most people don't see when staring at the picture of a successful person.

We once planned a weekend at the beach with friends during the renovation period. I opted to stay and work at the house that Friday night and leave Saturday morning while our friends partied. I didn't brood about it. There was no need. I was doing what was necessary to get it completed. Anytime someone tells me I'm lucky or that it must be nice to have money, I tell them this story (or a similar one, I have plenty). Then I'll ask them:

What's your level of commitment? What are willing to do to achieve your dreams?

I have often found that you don't have to 'go the extra mile' to be successful. Sometimes it's as simple as working a few extra hours on a Friday night.

Slowly I turn….

I wasn't quite setting a record pace early in my real estate career. After finishing Linwood I made a goal for myself to purchase 100 apartments within 2 years. It wasn't until March of 1997 that I bought my second investment property. The MD Housing Fund had another property for sale at 300 South Newkirk St. with an asking price of $45,000. After looking at many of their sales, I figured out that their asking price was the value after improvements were made. Therefore, I decided to offer a net price of $31,000.

To avoid the red tape of another 203(k) loan, I actually changed the price to $36,000 on the contract with the seller to credit me $5,000 at settlement for repair & improvement money. This simple way to get a credit at settlement would work wonders for my future deals. I also insisted that I be a co-borrower with my wife on this deal. Since the dollar amounts involved were small and we had 1 rental under our belts the lender agreed. This was my stepping stone to rebuilding my credit after the bankruptcy.

This property didn't need as much work as the first and in a short period of time I had it rented for $600 a month with a monthly payment of $300. I did run into a headache when trying to complete the backyard. This was a typical city rowhouse with a concrete pad for a backyard and a cinderblock wall lining the perimeter. The cement was busted apart and a large section of the wall was missing. Someone had probably plowed into it with a car years ago and the previous owner neglected to rebuild it.

I had to make over 30 calls before I found a mason that returned my call & sounded coherent (Quick Hint: Always keep a current Yellow Pages directory in your car. With a cell phone you become a mobile unit ready to get things done immediately). After starting the job and getting about half of it done the mason suddenly disappeared. I had to call him a dozen times & eventually threaten to take him to court if he didn't finish the job. This is one reason why I treat any good contractor like gold. I don't cherry pick when it comes to getting good help. I know a lot of investors who will constantly beat up a contractor for the lowest price and to have the job done immediately. I believe I get better results by finding good people who work for a reasonable price, and then I throw them all of my business. It doesn't take long until I'm getting their best price because of the volume of business they're getting from me.

"Go against me, and I will win. Go with me, and we will win"
-Bruno Siva

CHAPTER 4

Okay, so by now we have moved out of the apartment, own two rental properties and I am working 40 hours a week selling computer software. Christine was making good money as a speech therapist and there was enough positive cash flow from the rentals to cover a car payment. And of course, I was still commanding a powerful $7.21 an hour plus commission working in my full-time cubicle.

If you're stepping forward, you might as well jump....

Around the beginning of 1997 I came across a book by Dodge Woodson called <u>Rehabbing Your Way to Riches</u>. It was written in 1992 and most of the contents were the usual stuff I'd read before. Fortunately for me, I like to read almost anything about real estate because I know that just one idea can make a huge difference.

I might have read this somewhere else in the past, but there was one section of his book that leapt out at me. It was a chapter on locating good deals. One of the marketing tools he discussed would become my staple for the next several years. It would allow me to amass millions in real estate. In fact, almost every property I purchased from now on would be the result of direct mail. I told you this was simple.

I decided to roam around a couple of key areas in Baltimore that I thought would become good long-term values. After focusing on two neighborhoods, I drove up and down a couple of the streets and wrote down the addresses (first address on block & last address on block). I then went home and connected online to the Maryland Department for Tax Assessment. This gave me free access to a database of every property in the state. From there I would enter the street name and scroll through page after page of individual addresses. Each time I found one I wanted I would have to bring it up separately and print that page. I would do this bleary eyed into the night.

After accumulating a couple of hundred pages, each with a property owner's address, I would create mailing labels on the computer for each one. Keep in mind that I was mailing to the property owner's address, not necessarily the actual property itself. In any large city there are thousands of properties that are owned by non-owner occupants.

I would then affix a label to a #10 envelope along with my return address, stamp it, and place inside a simple one page letter stating that I buy property in that area & if they are thinking of selling to contact me. After a trip to the post office with about 4 grocery bags filled with letters, I would fill the outgoing mail slot to the brim.

I knew there were direct mail companies that could do all of this for me, but at the time I couldn't afford their services. Just because I couldn't afford to have someone else do it, did that stop me? My only cost outside of postage and a box of paper & envelopes was my time late at night. Again, what are you willing to do to succeed?

You might be wondering why someone would call a stranger if they're looking to sell their property. Why wouldn't they list it with a broker, put an ad in the paper, or put a sign on the property instead?

Good question, but there are a lot of answers. Some properties have problems that drive away other buyers. Sometimes there's not enough equity to afford a brokers commission. I know it's hard to believe in 2007, but it wasn't very long ago that property owners were desperate to get rid of their property.

Into the big leagues we go….

A few months after buying the house on Newkirk Street I received a phone call from an older gentleman named Charles. He had received one of my letters and was looking to sell a 5 unit building overlooking a reservoir near mid-town Baltimore.

The building was in an area that I didn't particularly like. It wasn't a 'war zone' or a completely dilapidated neighborhood, but it was 'on the edge' as we say in these parts. What attracted me was the uniqueness of the building and its location. It resembled an old colonial brick house with a slate roof and a stately appearance. The lot had grass on three sides and a ten car parking pad in the rear. The best part was that there was a large high-rise apartment building right next door and another high-rise directly behind it. Both buildings were well staffed and had 24-hour security. The total monthly rent was $2,400 plus there was a coin operated washer & dryer in the basement that took in another $100 a month. The asking price was $100,000.

What made this deal really work for me was that the owner had a decent chunk of equity in the building, approximately $30,000. I decided to offer his purchase price, but he would have to hold a second mortgage for his 30k in equity. I was reasonably sure I could get a first mortgage for 70k. My total monthly payment for both loans was $1,150. I had to use some savings and borrow off the credit card again to get the $6,300 in closing costs for settlement. The basement was flooding badly whenever it rained, so I spent $1,200 to have a drainage ditch dug around the inside perimeter of the basement and empty into a sump pump.

Quick note-

I always include a right of first refusal anytime a seller holds a second mortgage for me. There are times when a seller gets tired of slow monthly payments and wants a lump sum of cash instead. When they try to sell their note, usually at less than the full value, the right of first refusal forces them to come back to me for approval. I can then approve it or better yet reduce my debt by negotiating to buy the note back for the same discount.

There were several long-term tenants in the building, one vacancy and one Section 8 tenant named Roland. This guy was a pistol. It's amazing to me that people receiving subsidized rent, paid by the government, would have much to complain about. By this time I had a pager so that tenants could contact me and a PO Box for collecting the rent. I always tried to keep the business separate from my personal life. Roland would leave the wildest messages for me, usually late at night. His best performance was when he called about 1:00am complaining that there were rats getting into his apartment (bear in mind his unit was a small one bedroom about 7 feet above ground level). After leaving his usual rant of sporadic sentences he finished by saying he wasn't at home but that I should call him at 416-764.... and then he hung up.

Along with his phone calls, chasing him down for his share of the rent was always a headache. The Section 8 program would pay for $400 of his rent with the remaining $50 to be paid by Roland. Each month I would have to hunt for him. I worked just as hard to collect that $50 as I did collecting from others who owed a full months rent.

I had a few other slow payers in the building and being so new to real estate, I would wait until the fifth day of the month before taking action. Not knowing the tenant/landlord laws very well, my first course of action was to type a late notice and leave it under their door. If that brought no response, I would then leave a notice telling them to vacate in 30 days.

Just like a teacher who learns from their students, so these tenants taught me how to landlord. And landlord I did. By word of mouth I learned of a company that catered to landlords with non-paying tenants. In fact, I discovered that there were many such companies around town. For a fee of $7 plus court costs, they would file eviction paperwork with the city rent court and the sheriff was responsible for serving the tenant with the court date. After 7 days, I would call and have them file a Put-Out Notice which would then be forwarded to the sheriff for process. The sheriff would schedule a date and if the full amount wasn't paid, the sheriff, myself and a small crew would evict the tenant and put all of their personal belongings in the street (per Baltimore city law). The whole process usually took 30 days to complete.

For less than $50 and with 2 phone calls, I could legally have someone evicted for non-payment. This was a powerful arsenal in my real estate management handbag. The only recourse a tenant had was if the property was in disrepair and that they had given written notice to the landlord of the repairs needed.

It was around this time that I decided that no matter how great a new tenant seemed, no matter how nice they looked, no matter how nice their clothes or what type of job they had, from this point forward every time I signed a lease I made it crystal clear when the rent was due and the exact consequences of non-payment. I would explain it matter-of-factly as if it was written in stone. For me the rent is due on the 1st of the month, it's late if paid after the 5th (5% late fee) and I file eviction paperwork if not received by the 10th.

Keep in mind that when you're just starting out, you may be new to this arena but many of these tenants are seasoned pro's. You're not a large indifferent management company with thousands of apartments; you're a 'one person show' trying to get something started. If they sense that you are incompetent or spineless, they will string you along for quite a ride. Hey, even a veteran landlord gets strung along once in awhile.

I'm not trying to seem braggadocios when it comes to evicting people, but you must never forget that this is a business. You don't have to be ruthless, but if you don't have the stomach to occasionally evict a family, or a single mom, then maybe you should stay away from rentals and focus on another area of real estate. At the end of the day if you've acted responsibly, honestly and within your values you should not have a problem running the management side of rental property.

Let's see where we are….

By now I have 7 units spread across 3 properties. The total monthly rents are $3,675 and the monthly payments (PITI-principal,interest,taxes,insurance) total $1,840, leaving me a monthly cash flow of $1,835 less any maintenance, vacancy, management costs, etc. Not bad. Especially when you consider that I was making $1,100 a month after taxes working a full time job.

This is where some people start to slide. They see a little extra money coming in each month and start shopping for a new car or a vacation to Cancun. What did I do? Do you even have to ask?

That's right. I kept my head down, stayed focused, and plowed ahead. My goal was to have 100 apartments. I think it's important to remind you that I was doing this for a variety of reasons: to provide for my wife & future family, to prove that I wasn't a failure for not going to college and to become the kind of person & have the material things that I dreamed about.

Not back then, and not to this day, would you overhear me bragging or extolling my 'real estate brilliance'. On the contrary, I am reluctant to discuss my business unless someone asks me about it first. I know many people in real estate that can't wait to bore you for twenty minutes about all their great deals and all their 'pearls of wisdom'. I always politely excuse myself from these braggarts as soon as possible.

You should have clear and solid goals for your business and personal life. Never let one of them be vanity.

CHAPTER 5

What did they say in that infomercial….

During the fall of 1997 I was staying on top of my rentals and looking for more. I decided to do another direct mail campaign in a different part of town. Within days I had all sorts of people calling. The first one to strike my interest was a guy named Tom. He owned a nice three story building in a great white collar neighborhood called Charles Village. Located at 2737 Saint Paul Street, this property had one apartment on each floor with the rents totaling $1,600 a month. With one steam boiler supplying heat to all the radiators and one hot water tank, the expenses were high since Tom had the heat & hot water included in the rent. In the coming years I would come up with a great way to recoup my expense for these things and at the same time not lose a single tenant.

It's amazing to think that many of these grand Victorian rowhomes in Baltimore were built as single family residences. Even more amazing was that Tom owned this building free and clear (no mortgage). His recently deceased father had paid $5,000 for the house fifty years ago and the loan had long since been paid. I also discovered, through casual conversation, that Tom was recently retired and had already bought a house near the beach. In other words, I assumed he didn't need an all cash deal at settlement.

I decided to offer $100,000 with Tom receiving $50,000 at settlement (less closing costs) and he would hold a second mortgage for $50,000 payable in the following schedule:

Year 1	$250/month
Year 2	$300/month
Year 3	$400/month
Year 4	$550/month
Year 5	$650/month

(interest only payments with no prepayment penalty)

After the property was under contract I immediately got to work securing a first mortgage. Lenders love these types of deals because their precious first mortgage is well secured- wouldn't you love to lend $50,000 if you knew it was secured with this type of property?

In reality, what I did was get a first mortgage for $60,000 and Tom still took back a second mortgage for $50,000. Technically this looks like overfinancing because my purchase price was 100k and my total debt would be 110k. Why would I do something like this? I can give you several great reasons:

1. Regardless of the purchase price I knew the appraised value of the building was at least $130,000.
2. The additional $10,000 in debt would be a credit to me at settlement. After closing costs, I left settlement with a check for $5,928.18. Not only was this a classic 'no money down' deal, but I actually walked away from that closing with tax free money in hand.
3. With the way I structured the payments of the second mortgage, I knew I would have positive cash flow for the first couple of years. After that I could refinance and lump both mortgages into one new loan at a lower interest rate.

This is about as good as it gets in real estate. I had instant equity- I could've instantly sold that building and made $20,000. I had instant positive cash flow because the building was not in need of any major repairs. Best of all, I had instant cash. Buying a house, not bringing any money to settlement, and leaving with a check has got to be one of the greatest high's you can have in this business.

Two things happened right after the sale that I wasn't too pleased about. First, the hot water tank went up & had to be replaced quickly. Second, the tenants on the 1st floor vacated their apartment and skipped out on that month's rent payment. I wasn't surprised since I noticed they had little furniture and a messy home.

I know a lot of people who would've called Tom to complain bitterly. How dare he sell a building knowing there were bad tenants and blah, blah ,blah. They might even demand some sort of compensation for the hot water tank and the loss of rent. Some might even withhold the first couple of payments on Tom's second mortgage as compensation.

What did I do? Nothing.

I solved the problems, re-rented the apartment and kept moving forward. I knew I had gotten a good deal on this property. I also thought it wise to keep Tom happy and in his 'good graces' so to speak. Maybe Tom would know another seller and pass along my name. I had kept to the terms of our deal and bought his property with no headaches. I figured other sellers would be more than happy to do business with me.

I didn't know how right I was.

Quick Note- In order to get that vacant unit ready for another tenant I had to paint the entire apartment. Short on cash, I would leave my full time job at 5:00pm and drive thirty minutes into the city and work for several hours every night. Because the walls were curved where they met the ceiling, I had to paint literally every square inch to make it look right.

Just remember that some times you must do whatever it takes to get a job done when you're working for yourself. Upon completion I was able to rent the apartment to a fantastic woman who gave me zero headaches for the next couple of years.

CHAPTER 6

Keep that train a movin'….

By the beginning of 1998, I was officially a real estate 'player'. I had 2 single family rowhouses, a 5 unit building and a 3 unit building. That's when Charles, the seller of the 5 unit building, called me again.

By now he had been receiving payments on his second mortgage for over six months. There's one thing I always did when it came to owner financing and I think it was critical to my overall success- I always paid them first each month. No matter what my cash flow situation, I always made sure anyone who was personally holding a mortgage & getting payments from me would never have to come looking for their money. This is a key component, a cornerstone of any business- trust. They knew they could set their watch by my timely payments, month after month.

Charles called me because he had a 7 unit building, in a great neighborhood, and he was tired of being a landlord. The building had been renovated ten years earlier and was a Baltimore classic- high ceilings with crown molding, plaster walls, intricately decorated fireplace mantels, old-style oversized doors, etc. Each apartment had been modernized with central air, upgraded electric, dishwashers and garbage disposals. Best of all, each unit was self-contained meaning that each tenant paid for their own utilities. My only utility expense was the water.

After many years of being a landlord, Charles wanted out badly. He was willing to sell the building for just enough to pay off his mortgage, approximately $180,000 (to give you an idea how good this was, that same property today would sell for about $700,000). After writing a contract my first priority was to contact the current lender and see if I could assume the loan.

Fortunately, the mortgage was held by a local bank that kept all of its lending in-house (they didn't package their loans and resell them on the secondary market). I requested an appointment with one of the VP's in charge of commercial lending and presented them with our contract. They had no problem letting me assume the loan, provided that I had someone co-sign with me. In reality they could see that, despite my youth, I owned other rentals and had a handle on what I was doing. But banks will always squeeze for as much security as they can get. I really didn't want to, but I decided to ask my father to co-sign the loan with me. I could've asked someone I worked with or I could've structured other financing, but asking my dad was honestly just easier. He wouldn't have to put up a dime of his own money & it could also provide some write-off for his taxes.

One mistake I made was trying to avoid transfer taxes at closing by assuming the partnership that owned the building. I spent so much money having an attorney draw up the paperwork that it would've been easier, and just as costly, to have bought the building in a new name.

Regardless, in a short period of time I was the new owner of an enormous property with tremendous cash flow. With gross rents of over \$3,500 a month, I was netting over \$1,000 a month after all expenses were paid! Since there was no need for a 2nd mortgage & no way to 'over finance' the property, I had to really squeeze my savings and came to settlement with a check for \$6,772.58. With such great cash flow, though, it didn't take very long to get my money back.

It can't be this easy, can it?

Sure it can! Let's keep going.

CHAPTER 7

Remember in Chapter 5 how I described purchasing a nice 3 unit building at 2737 Saint Paul Street and that I actually walked away from closing with a check in my hand.

And remember how in Chapter 6 I said that one of my keys to success was always paying a personal mortgage holder first each month (I paid all my mortgages each month, but I made sure to pay Tom & Charles before I mailed a check to an impersonal third party like Wells Fargo).

Well....

During the summer of 1998, about 4 months after buying Tom's 3 unit building, I received a call from Jim, Tom's brother. It seems that their father had left them each a 3 unit building, with no mortgage, on the same block. The rents at 2725 Saint Paul were a little lower and at first I tried to negotiate a lower price than what I paid to his brother, but after some resistance I decided it was still a great deal and I made an identical offer to Jim (I will discuss in detail in the Bonus sections how the pro's determine an offer price).

Almost like magic, I now owned two 3 unit buildings on the same block with good income and good tenants. The loan for this deal wasn't the same as the other property and I ended up paying additional points & closing costs to get it done. In the end I walked away from settlement owning a 3 unit building, with cash flow, and a check made out to me for $3,002.15 that was tax free.

It may seem like magic, or that I was lucky, but was I really? I think I created my own luck. Success doesn't happen all at once. You don't just leap to the top of the mountain. It's small, consistent actions done every week that will produce results.

In this case I:

Drove around neighborhoods until I found one I liked.

Looked up all the owners, one at a time, and created a mailing list.

Drafted a letter, folded it and placed it inside hundreds of envelopes.

Responded to anyone who called me as a result of receiving one of my letters.

Picked through the pile until I found the diamonds.

Negotiated deals, hustled for financing & made sure I closed as agreed.

Paid my personal mortgage holders first with zero headaches for them.

None of these actions were exceptionally difficult. In fact, most of it was pretty simple as I've stated before. But most people won't put this much effort into creating the life they want. They'll spend more time planning a vacation than they will planning their financial future.

But not you and me, right?

CHAPTER 8

By the summer of 1998, I was completely exhausted with my day job. Despite the fact that I had moved up to a 30k salary, I was caught in a vicious circle selling computer software. With each installation there would be one more customer with something to complain about, one more programming headache, one more fellow worker ticked off about something. I decided it was time to move on.

Since I was doing well with my rentals, I thought it a good idea to get a full time job in the real estate industry. There are always lots of ads for residential property management in our area, but the pay is low and the work is tedious at best. By now I had been managing my own properties for a couple of years and could do it in my sleep. But then I saw an ad for commercial property management. Unlike other CPM ads, this one did not require a degree or anything that I didn't possess.

After a few phone calls a meeting was arranged with chief of operations for Boxer Property, a privately owned Texas based company with dozens of class B commercial buildings in numerous cities. They were about to close on a package of eight buildings in downtown Baltimore and needed full staffing for on-site management, leasing and maintenance.

I thought my interview had gone well. I had presented myself as ambitious and a straightforward businessman. Even though I had no formal training or education, especially in commercial management, I used my small portfolio of real estate to my advantage. What did it matter that I didn't have a Bachelors Degree or whatever; I knew how to be tough on rent collection, how to evict a non-payer and how to repair a building. The dollar amounts might obviously be different, but the process was the same. I left the interview with a good feeling and looked forward to a phone call.

A few days later I got a call from them saying they would be back in town and would like a second meeting. I thought for sure that they were offering me a position and they did- except it wasn't the one I had applied for.

At my 2nd interview they offered me a job as a leasing consultant. This is someone that meets with prospective tenants, negotiates the lease, etc. I told them that I had not applied for the leasing job and that I knew I could do well as a property manager, and I politely left. They looked a little surprised to say the least, but I was under no pressure. I wasn't crazy about my current job, but I wasn't ready to jump out a window either. The cash flow from the rentals was good so I decided to keep my options open and look for another opportunity.

"Three outstanding qualities make for success: judgment, industry, health. And the greatest of these is judgment."
-William Maxwell Aitken

Take a chance....

About a month after passing up the leasing consultant offer, my wife suggested that I call them and see if anything new had developed. I was a little skeptical, and probably a little fearful of calling, but thought 'what the heck'. Maybe they had yet to fill the management position and were pressed for options.

I called and sure enough that job was still available. After a third meeting I accepted an offer as a commercial property manager for Boxer Property's Baltimore office.

For the first time in my life I felt in control. I was directing my life instead of being a victim of circumstances and excuses. Starting in 1996 without any money or college degree, I had by the end of 1998 a job in management, owned 20 rental units and best of all I had accomplished a major goal of replacing my wife's income with rental income. This came in very handy when she gave birth in September of 1998 to our first boy and was no longer bringing home a paycheck.

"Five minutes, just before going to sleep, given to a bit of directed imagination regarding achievement possibilities of the morrow, will steadily and increasingly bear fruit, particularly if all ideas of difficulty, worry or fear are resolutely ruled out and replaced by those of accomplishment and smiling courage"
-Frederick Pierce

Real estate, Texas style….

Upon giving a month's notice that I would no longer be pushing computer software, I spent all of January 1999 immersing myself in real estate management training in Houston. I think being away from my daily routine and in a different 'culture' really allowed me to focus my attention on learning as much as possible. Boxer Property had a formal and professional approach to real estate and was a perfect match for my businesslike approach to it as well.

For several weeks I worked with one of their best managers and learned the commercial world. Operating an office building isn't really that much different than managing residential rentals. You seek good tenants and stay tough on rent collection, keep the exterior & common areas clean and get your vacant units ready for occupancy ASAP. A great benefit of working for a large company is having an accounting staff in-house. Over the months that followed, I educated myself on accounting principles and its value is immeasurable for what I do now. Whether you're wholesaling, retailing or renting property, having a solid accounting of your income & expenses is critical. You can't build a business or make sound decisions without good Profit & Loss statements, balance sheets and accurate information.

Into the fire we go....

I returned home at the end of January only to find myself in a whirlwind. My wife had been with our brand new baby boy for weeks and needed some time for herself. I had several vacant units that needed attention and a few slow paying tenants that needed to be shaken. Before I started my new position, the Operations Manager for the Baltimore Office was fired for incompetence and it was now up to me and the other property manager to run 8 buildings and hundreds of tenants.

So what was my next move? You guessed it; I bought 2 more buildings! Actually, I had put these under contract prior to my Texas trip. It was now time to take them to settlement.

As for my vacancies I decided to hire a contractor to go in and get them ready for occupancy. I really didn't have the money for this, but I could only juggle so many things at this point and slinging a paint brush till 11pm wasn't one of them. Intellectually I know that I'll always make more money with my mind than with my hands, but the reality was that money was tight with only one salary and some cash flow from the rentals. By having someone else work on my vacant units, I was able to spend some quality time with my family and keep my sanity.

"Anyone can hold the helm when the sea is calm".
-Publilius Syrus

One of the 2 buildings I had under contract was a large 7 unit building in the same neighborhood as the 7 unit I had purchased a year before. Located at 221 W. Lanvale Street, this building contained small apartments and was in great condition. Prior to writing an offer I had met with the property manager and walked through each unit.

After the meeting I was given a current Operating Statement and the rent roll.

This is where a healthy dose of common sense can work wonders. Whenever you're fortunate enough to be provided any type of financial statements (not too common on small individual properties) try to see the big picture. This person was selling and I don't blame him; he was losing money every year even though he had a great property with over 40k a year in gross rents! Where was the money going?

Along with an eight percent management fee, the management company was also charging a 10% 'supervisory fee'. This is charged whenever work is being 'supervised' in the building (painting, cleaning, etc.). There was a maintenance contract charge for $59.95 and a 'services' charge for $395. One charge that really caught my attention and initially put me on guard to really examine these numbers was the charge for locks & keys- $473. I distinctly remembered the manager fumbling with a jangle of keys as we toured the building. Not only were all the locks different, some apartment doors had 2 separate keys for the same door. For a small building like this you could've re-keyed and put everything on one master key for that price. This was a great example why you should always manage your own properties, at least initially, so that you have an idea of what the real costs may be.

The one negative aspect to the building was that all the units shared a common hot water tank and radiator heating system. Both of the systems were brand new and cost the owner almost $10,000 to install. The downside, just like my other multi-unit buildings, was that I as the landlord would be stuck with the hot water & heating costs. Sometimes it's only a small annoying expense, but in a property of this size the costs could be staggering. Their statement showed $897 for electricity, $4,160 for natural gas and $711 for water annually; that's over 14% of the rent gross rent right off the top! (Within a year I devised a way to eliminate the gas & electric expense from my books completely and not lose a single tenant- more on this later).

After paying all of these expenses plus the mortgage, this poor owner was forced to advance $7,500 that year to the management company to stay in the black. This owner had a great low maintenance building occupied with good white collar tenants and he was losing his shirt. He had received one of my letters and called me so I reviewed everything and made an offer.

My offering price was $190,000 with the seller to hold a $60,000 second mortgage with interest only payments all due in 5 years. I also asked him to pay $5,000 towards my closing costs, and he accepted. I approached the same local bank that had allowed me to assume the note on the other 7 unit building for a $130,000 loan. They had all my financial information already so it was a quick & simple solution.

I was a bit surprised at settlement when the seller showed up with his attorney. He had not been involved in the signing of the contract and had not been mentioned up until this point. I was even more surprised when I saw the first copy of the settlement sheet- it stated that I was to pay over $2,000 in closing costs. I didn't bother bringing any certified funds to closing because my calculations showed that I was walking away from this deal with a check, not giving a check.

Sure enough, the title company had failed to include the $5,000 credit toward my closing costs that the seller agreed to pay. His attorney tried to block this, but I quickly pulled my copy of the contract with the original signatures on it. Any time I add something to a standard real estate contract, it's on a separate sheet of paper and written in clear & simple language. Never try to hide what you're doing! I take great pains to keep everything as simple and open as possible to avoid just these types of situations. Within a minute the attorney saw that they had no argument and we proceeded with the sale. When you know you're right, hold your ground no matter who the players are. The only reason someone will bring in legal counsel at the last minute is to intimidate you.

After this was re-calculated, I left that settlement with over $3,400 in my pocket and a great deal. I had $4,300 in gross monthly rent and my total payments for both loans was $1,700. Even after deducting the property taxes, insurance, expenses (which I sliced) I still had a tremendous cash flow off this one property.

And remember, this owner called *me*. I didn't coerce him into any deal and he wasn't wringing his hands in despair at settlement. This was a classic example of an absentee owner who was in over his head.

Back on the day job....

Life at Boxer Property was fast paced. This was the height of the dot-com venture capital explosion and our leasing department was going gangbusters. Managing four buildings across several blocks kept me moving all day. I was rarely sitting behind a desk and my typical company cell phone usage was close to 1,200 minutes a month.

Standard company hours were Monday through Friday, 8:30am to 5:30pm.

My typical day started in downtown Baltimore at about 7:00am, sometimes even earlier. Parking on the street was tight and I had contractors buzzing everywhere improving the buildings and doing tenant build-out (paint, carpet, general construction to get a vacant office ready for occupancy). Sometimes I would have so much activity that the contractors were tying up the elevators and leaving dust everywhere. Some tenants even complained to the corporate office about the crazed level of activity. Keep in mind that many of our tenants were attorneys who liked having an office within a block of the main courthouse and they were accustomed to the previous absentee ownership. The previous owners had deferred maintenance for years and had entire floors of buildings completely vacant.

I thought it fascinating that this private company had hundreds of millions of dollars worth of commercial property and yet their business model was very similar to my own. In fact, many of their purchases were structured just like my first investment property. You buy a property for 'X', but get a loan for X + 20% more. Then fix up the property ASAP, have an inspection by the lender, and get your 20% money back after the improvements are made. The numbers were different, but the strategy was identical.

I found managing a medium sized commercial building fairly simple. I eliminated costs wherever I could. I would eliminate unused telephone or fax lines, install energy efficient lighting, stay on top of contractors & make sure jobs were getting done on time. The lessons in cost control were invaluable. In the winter many of the buildings were heated by old-fashioned steam radiators. In most older cities there are huge underground pipes pumping steam into the basements where it is controlled and fed throughout the building. One property had a faulty control and it wasn't discovered until I received a $30,000 invoice for that month's steam supply. It was a good reminder that a little preventive care can save a lot of headache & money down the road.

As for dealing with commercial tenants, most of my relationships were cordial and professional. It was a great training ground for honing my 'people skills'. There was an older gentleman who was a former state attorney for Maryland that would yell like a lunatic anytime he had a problem. Once, when the air conditioning on his floor was being repaired, he called the receptionist every other minute until I was in the office. Picking up the phone, I listened to him rant non-stop for several minutes. Whenever I tried to speak, he would start yelling. I decided to remain dead silent and after another five minutes of yelling he wore himself out. Realizing he wasn't going to get me angry, he hung up the phone.

I always try to play off whomever I'm dealing with when negotiating or resolving a situation. I call it wearing whatever hat is necessary. Some people respond better when you ask them politely to do something. Other people shrug off politeness and respond only when yelled at. Still others need to be flattered before you can get them moving. I think being flexible like this has helped my success quite a bit.

Overall, I was cruising and having a good time. I was an active decision maker for the company's Baltimore portfolio, engaged in corporate meetings via tele-conference, making friendly jabs at the accounting department and enjoying the 'water cooler' company gossip.

CHAPTER 9

A month after buying my second 7 unit building I purchased a nice 3 unit building from an out of state owner named John. Originally, John and his wife had bought the property and lived in the 1st floor apartment while renting out the other 2 units. After a job transfer (and a new baby), they now lived over an hour away and were not too thrilled about absentee landlording.

John was an accountant and a bright guy, but it was amazing how long it took to purchase this house. It wasn't a negotiation over price; my initial offer of $95,000 was okay with him. I had even asked him to pay $4,000 towards my closing costs and that was okay too. Through our conversations I sensed that he wasn't a 'people person' and perhaps a little untrusting of a stranger. This was perfectly understandable. After all, he had received one of my direct mail letters and now he was about to bind himself to a legally enforceable document.

At this stage of the negotiation I decided to do 2 things. First, I encouraged him to seek legal counsel and have the contract looked over. I use a standard Maryland Association of Realtors purchase agreement and it's very unambiguous. Any attorney will modify it slightly, but I knew this wouldn't be a problem. And are you ready for this? The second thing I did was invite him over to my house for dinner! This may seem crazy to some people, and maybe it was a little crazy but so what! I wanted him to feel comfortable dealing with me and I knew that if he saw where I lived (a modest 3 bedroom townhouse at that time) it would give him a warmer, fuzzy feeling about me. I was a real person, with a real wife, living where I said I did in a real house. I wasn't trying to take advantage of him so I felt that I had absolutely nothing to hide.

Within 2 weeks Christine & I entertained John and his wife at our house. We had a relaxed conversation and the deal was finally done.

Swimming with the sharks....

With the contract signed in February 1999, I purchased 2644 N. Calvert Street the following month. With $95,000 borrowed from a private lender, a $4,000 credit from the seller and the credit for rents paid in March, my total out of pocket cash needed to buy this nice building was $631. John, the seller, *paid* $9,680. That's right, he paid money to sell his house. Why? Only John can answer that for sure. Maybe he felt it was the best he was going to do. Although the price was $95,000, his first mortgage was a little over $100,000. Adding the $4,000 credit he gave me plus other miscellaneous closing costs left him in the hole. But remember, he's an accountant and maybe was looking at this picture from a completely different perspective. He was happy & so was I.

Although I had used seller held financing on other deals, this was my first time using a private money lender. I had gotten this person's name from a title company and had called to see if he had any interest in financing this deal. After his appraiser did a 'drive-by' look at the property, he offered to finance the entire purchase price at 14% interest, with monthly interest only payments and the balance to be paid off within one year. Did I accept? You bet I did. If a deal hinges on getting the absolute best interest rate, then you had better check your numbers. If you're buying at the right price the interest rate should only be a small consideration in the big picture. I'll discuss proper valuation and financing in greater detail in the Bonus sections, but a good deal will always remain solid regardless of the interest rate if the property is purchased correctly.

The third time is always a charm....

Do you remember Charles, the owner of the 5 unit and 7 unit buildings that I purchased at great prices? Well, once again the power of trust was pushing my success right along. I had continued my policy of always, and I do mean *always*, paying my private lenders first every month. Charles had taken back a second mortgage on one property and an unsecured lien on the other and had been receiving my payments like clockwork.

So when the time came to sell 2418 Saint Paul Street, who do you think he called first? This was actually a small commercial building with three tenants and parking for 10 cars right in the middle of the city. I wasn't ecstatic about dealing with commercial tenants, but with my experience at Boxer I felt I could adjust and handle whatever came up. The real selling point for this property was in the numbers, like any great deal, and this one was sure to be a winner.

Charles was asking $140,000, had a 100k mortgage that had to be paid off and he was willing to finance the 40k difference. Here's exactly how I structured the deal: I made the purchase price $165,000 with the seller to credit me 25k at settlement. In addition, at settlement we created a note for 39k payable over ten years. I then approached my lender that had financed my other larger multi-unit buildings and applied for a 75% loan to value based on the 165k purchase price. This meant that the bank was going to give me a mortgage for a little over

123k. With the 25k credit and the 39k second mortgage, after deducting closing costs I walked away from this settlement with a check for almost $20,000 (tax free, I might add)! I also had about $500 a month in positive cash flow from the first day I owned it.

Now, why would I mortgage a property for $162,000 (123k 1st mortgage and the 39k 2nd mortgage) when the seller was only asking for $140,000?

Because I recognized value. It's absolutely critical that you know the values in the areas you are investing. You don't have to be exact, but you should be able to ballpark it without much effort. If the numbers are so tight that a $5,000 error will have you questioning if you should pursue a deal, chances are you're going to lose money or break even at best. I knew without blinking that this building was worth more than 140k and the bank appraisal confirmed my belief when they estimated it at $175,000!

'Only in quiet waters do things mirror themselves undistorted.
Only in a quiet mind is adequate perception of the world.'
-Hans Margolius

CHAPTER 10

A month after I bought the commercial building from Charles, I received a call from a guy named Rick. He, too, had received one of my simple letters and said that he wanted to sell some property he owned- 8 multi-unit buildings with a total of 28 apartments! I couldn't drive to his office fast enough.

Rick had a job with the government and owned a bunch of rentals on the side. He was in the middle of a messy divorce and needed to sell off most of his properties. I left his office with a copy of the rent roll and immediately set out to inspect the buildings. With gross rents of over $11,000 a month for these units, I was about to double my portfolio overnight.

I quickly had the properties under contract, with great prices, and called my private hard money lender. He had his appraiser drive by each building and this is how the financing fell together: all eight buildings were to be bought at one time with eight separate settlement sheets for a total price of $575,000. My lender would give a total of $505,000 at 14% with a five year balloon. The balance of $70,000 would be held by the seller as 2nd mortgages on each building, thus making this yet another incredible nothing down deal.

With the financing in place I cruised through the title work, obtained insurance & completed the normal things done before buying property. Since we were settling at the beginning of the month the rents & security deposits would be credited to me and I was expecting to walk away from settlement with a large check. However, when I arrived at settlement I was reminded of the Golden Rule- "Those who own the gold get to make the rules!"

My hard money lender was charging me 4 points for this transaction for a total of $20,000. While waiting for the seller to arrive, I got on the phone with my lender and asked why he was charging me 4 points. He told me that this was his normal agreement and that the other transaction he did for me without points was an oversight. Now, maybe it was and maybe it wasn't. Maybe this private lender, whom I still had never met in person, was a lot smarter than I thought. Since he knew the rents, deposits and purchase price, he probably did a little calculating on his own and saw that I was going to walk away with cash from this deal. He politely, but assertively, let me know that I could back out at anytime and that there would be no hard feelings.

I decided very quickly that I was getting a great deal and kept the settlement moving forward. By the time the seller arrived, we had adjusted the settlement sheets and I was able to purchase all this real estate with just over $1,000 out of my pocket. After closing I spent a few days 'cleaning up'. There were keys that the seller gave me that didn't work, vacant units that had been on the rent roll as occupied and even a few supposed vacant units that were occupied with tenants. But I didn't care.

Overall, I was thrilled with what I had just accomplished.

'Live as if everything you do will eventually be known'
-Hugh Prather

Let's see how crazy we can go….

As you can imagine, at this point in my life there was never a dull moment. A typical day for me would go something like this:

- wake at 6:00am and head to the office to meet with contractors or do paperwork
- receive at least 1 angry call from a commercial tenant complaining that their office had not been cleaned the previous night
- receive a call from one of my tenants complaining that there's no hot water in the building

- fifteen minutes later, receive 3 more calls from the same building from the other tenants complaining about the lack of hot water
- walk some of the commercial buildings & get on my staff about the bathrooms, lobby's, etc. being unkempt
- get a call that someone is trapped in one of the elevators. Jog four blocks over and five blocks up to that building, run up flights of steps, lay on my stomach with my head poking down the elevator shaft and console whomever is trapped that we are doing everything we can to get them out. Twenty minutes later we get them out
- Christine calls just to see how my day is going
- meet contractor in the street & give them keys to my building so hot water problem can be resolved
- 9 to 5 workday is now over & have several options: put on work clothes and go patch & paint one of my vacant units, collect late rent from one or two of my tenants, or say the heck with all of it and go home & enjoy time with my family

Although it was quite frantic at times, I really did enjoy myself. Christine was home with our toddler being a full-time mom and I now had enough rental income each month that I didn't feel like a slave to the work force. I could start to see the light at the end of the tunnel and I knew my effort was going to pay off.

*'Start by doing what's necessary, then what's possible
and suddenly you are doing the impossible'*
-Saint Francis of Assisi

Most people don't remember specific days with the exception of birthdays, anniversaries and the like. But I remember March 22, 2000 quite well. We had just gotten back from a trip to Florida to visit Christine's parents and we were arguing over something dumb. In the middle of snipping at each other and from far left field, Christine told me she was pregnant with our second child. We quickly forgot our bickering and hugged for several minutes.

Later that night I decided to dial into the MLS and check for any new activity. Back in the late nineties and through 2001, there wasn't this frenetic pace to real estate that exists today. Typical properties languished on the market for months at a time, often being withdrawn without any offers.

With a renewed sense of purpose, that night I came across an 8 unit building that had been listed for sale that very same day. Each unit was separately metered for heat, hot water and electric. The building was in need of some serious TLC. Three of the apartments were vacant & one of the tenants was about to be evicted. It was a bank foreclosure and the asking price was $117,500. She was perfect and she was about to be mine.

I offered $100,000 with a contingency that I could secure a loan. The bank countered at 112k, but I held firm. Again, this was in the year 2000 and the building needed work. Within 24 hours the bank had accepted my deal and I started churning in my buying mode, as usual. I immediately contacted Columbia Bank (my local lender on the two 7 unit buildings), wrote a list of repairs, and after a brief visit to the property by the lender the financing was in place. This was my first deal where I would have to put a significant amount down, do the repairs, and then get a draw from the bank for the completed work.

With a little creative borrowing off a credit card and cashing in my wife's small IRA, I was able to swing the $25,000 down payment and closing costs. Most people wouldn't consider doing this, but I was bent on building an empire. The appraiser had estimated the improved value of the building to be $200,000 after the $25,000 in repairs was completed. This meant that the bank would loan me 75k at settlement towards the purchase, then reimburse me 25k for the repairs making the total loan 100k. Having only a 50% loan to value was extremely good for the bank. What I should have done differently was increase my repair estimate by 100%. That way I could have done the repairs and been reimbursed for the 25k down payment, thus making it a nothing down deal after the work was done and I got the escrowed draw money.

This oversight in how I structured the repair money would squeeze me for the rest of the year. We were coming off a brutally cold winter and natural gas prices had spiked 20% over previous years. This was huge to me because most of my buildings were multi-units with one central heating and hot water system. The common practice was that the landlord paid for the heat and hot water in these types of properties. Since I was already $25,000 in the hole due to the down payment requirement on my last purchase, every month became a struggle to stay afloat while covering all the bills.

Out of necessity, and because I was using software that could easily keep track of it, I started to renew leases without raising the rent. Instead, I reasoned with each of my tenants that it would be much cheaper for them in the long run if their rent stayed fixed and in return they would each contribute to the utility bill. For a three unit building the bill would be divided by 3, for a seven unit it was divided by 7, etc. Each month I would pay the bill then send each tenant a copy so they could see that everything was being done fairly and honestly. Some tenants would immediately send me a check, while others would simply include the payment with their next month's rent. It worked perfectly and not one tenant moved out or voiced much concern. In fact, this initiative had a double whammy effect. Not only was my utility cost now covered, but the bills started going down & my heating complaints practically vanished because now everyone had a vested interest in controlling the costs.

I'm going to wrap up this chapter on a somber note. There was a large down payment and lots of work to be done on the 8 unit building I had just purchased. If you have a multi-unit building with numerous vacant apartments and are planning to do significant improvements, more than likely the existing tenants will have to be moved out. If they're accustomed to run-down conditions, then they're probably not going to be the best tenants. There are exceptions, of course. I had one nice couple that kept their unit very clean & were eager to help in any way to improve the building. They would pick trash out of the front yard and keep the hallway clean.

A tenant on the second floor was not as receptive. Her apartment was absolutely filthy with mounds of clothes all over the place, dirty dishes overflowing in the kitchen sink and roaches running across the floor. The previous owner had become accustomed to her chronic late payments and the first time she tried it with me was her last. With a fair and even hand all my tenants knew where I stood on rent collection. I filed for an eviction and after the usual court procedure was played out, the sheriff was there a month later to serve the official eviction papers.

What broke my heart was that she had several small children living with her in these conditions. When the sheriff arrived, her oldest, a boy about 10 years old, was home on a school day by himself. I don't know if child protective services were contacted by the sheriff or what became of this family, but there is probably no worse feeling than evicting a single mother from her home. Evictions are a somber reminder that professional property management of your real estate is serious business.

CHAPTER 11

By the summer of 2000 I was behaving like a frenetic insect; every day was spent in reaction to events swirling about me. I now personally owned 70 apartments in 18 buildings. The other property manager at work had resigned and I was now in charge of not four but all eight commercial buildings owned by Boxer Property. My pregnant wife was home all day trying to keep up with our two year old as she steeled herself for another baby. On paper it looked as if I had life by the horns. I had a net worth of 1.2 million and a little over $33,000 a month in gross rents. Add to that a steady paycheck from my 9 to 5 job and one would assume that all was swell. But I was burning a candle on both ends and in the middle.

Something had to give. In addition to wanting Christine to be a stay-at-home mom, I was also buying rental property so that eventually I could strike out on my own and be my own boss. By June, that time had come. After composing a brief letter of resignation, I e-mailed a copy to the owner of Boxer, Andrew Segal, and forwarded a copy to the Chief of Operations.

Starting with a bankruptcy and working odd jobs like stacking soda in grocery stores, it had taken me four hard years to accomplish my goal. I had a million plus net worth, residual income from my rentals whether I worked every day or not, and a great family life to come home to every night. I had finally moved my life in a direction of momentum and possibility, instead of reaction and powerlessness.

And I was just thirty years old.

'When all is said and done, success without happiness is the worst kind of failure'
-Louis Binstock

Knowing that Boxer Property was in a bind without another local manager ready to take my place, I opted to forgo the standard practice of giving two weeks notice. Instead, I thought it would be more professional under the circumstances to wait sixty days before leaving. This would give them thirty days to find a replacement and another thirty days to train them if necessary. I've always found it better in business, and life in general, to do what's best and not necessarily what's considered standard practice.

I spent my remaining two months trying to tie up any loose ends as much as possible. Between delinquent rent collections, capital improvement projects, tenant construction projects and the daily grind of maintenance issues, there was plenty to keep me busy. Fortunately, a few weeks before my last scheduled day, the company was able to woo back the manager who had resigned earlier that year. This was a great relief to me as well as to Boxer. It would make my departure much less stressful for all of us; except of course my buddy who was left managing eight buildings by himself.

It was also around this time, about the end of July, that I received a call from Boxer's president, Andrew Segal. As I picked up the phone I naturally assumed that he just wanted to say so long & wish me well in the future. What he had to say simply floored me.

He wanted to know if I was interested in forming a partnership with him to buy residential property in Baltimore. I was a little apprehensive at first about this proposal. I'd always operated under the belief that if you can do business without a partner, then don't have any partners! But by aligning myself with Andrew I would be able to leverage my ability to buy property. It would allow me to negotiate with supreme confidence. Most of the standard real estate books profess the idea that money flows to good deals. While this may be true and I knew from my own experience that I could hustle up the money whenever a good deal came along, it would be much easier and faster if I was legitimately a cash buyer. Andrew could make this happen. With him as a partner I would be able to buy any good deal quickly with the least amount of unnecessary costs (appraisals, points, etc.).

The only part of this arrangement that I wasn't thrilled with was the split. It was 70/30 with me owning 30% of the new company. I did attempt to persuade Andrew to change this to 60/40 but he didn't budge. If I were him, I wouldn't have either. He was putting up all of the capital and therefore assuming most of the risk. At the time of this partnership, Andrew's commercial company, Boxer Property, had roughly $500 million in assets. I quickly came to my senses and realized that this new venture had enormous potential. If I owned 30% of a company that was even close to this size I would be ecstatic and very rich.

This deal had other tremendous perks as well. Until we became really established we could enjoy the benefit of Boxer's in-house accounting department and legal counsel. This would allow us to keep good monthly financials and deflect any legal matters without any additional costs.

Before we even had our arrangement in writing I started to beat the bushes looking for our first deal.

'Courage is the power to let go of the familiar'
-Raymond Lindquist

It didn't take very me very long. My last official day as an employee of Boxer Property was August 4, 2000. By August 15th, Andrew and I were standing amongst a small crowd gathered at 2427 Saint Paul Street. It was a 3 unit building with a small office on the first floor and three apartments above. One of the apartments was a complete disaster while the other two units just needed cosmetics (definition of a 'complete disaster'- it looked as if someone had lit a quarter stick of dynamite in the kitchen and then ran like hell).

I followed my usual auction bidding technique which was to wait until the bidding slowed down before swooping in at the last moment. When the auctioneer calls 'going once, going twice', that's precisely the time to jump in with a new bid. The last bidder is usually caught completely off guard and feeling deflated having come so close to winning that they typically get emotional and walk away. We picked up our first project for $32,500, which was a terrific price. After a 60k renovation, the three units would rent for $1,850 a month and the small office was a perfect location for our new venture.

By this time Andrew had come up with a great company name, Red Sculpture. He commissioned a Texas based artist to create a design. Obviously it's a bit difficult to describe art, but if you can imagine the cursive swirls in Coca-Cola turned vertically & painted firehouse red, then you've got an idea of the 'Red Sculpture'. After a small desktop model was crafted, within a few weeks I received a crate containing a ten foot high replica. I decided to mount it in the front yard of one of my buildings because it had a more visible location. What a stir that created. By that night I had received no less than a dozen vicious phone calls from the neighbors. One lady was actually upset simply because I had not gotten her approval before erecting it. I told her, as nicely as I could, that it was my damn yard and I would do whatever I wanted with it. After that first day the furor died off and it became a neighborhood novelty. It was like the one house in everyone's neighborhood with 10,000 glowing Christmas lights. People would go out of their way just to see it.

With a city so diverse in architecture as Baltimore, we decided it was important to bring a concept of 'sameness' to each building. The layout of each building and usually each apartment may be different, but we would focus on using the same paint, carpet and materials throughout our portfolio. The red sculpture ornament was just the right touch to set us apart.

Within a month I discovered yet another perk to being a partner with Andrew. I received a call from The Daily Record, Baltimore's legal and business newspaper. They wanted to do an interview to discuss our new business and take a picture of the sculpture. The October 26, 2000 issue has a great shot of the red sculpture in all its glory on the front page. I was a bit disappointed with the article. Almost everything that was written about me was wrong. Not that they said anything horrible, it's just that it wasn't quite accurate. Regardless, we were making waves and finding more deals.

CHAPTER 12

Before the renovation work on Red Sculpture's first purchase was complete, I located a nice 8 unit building in the same neighborhood. It was actually right behind one of my buildings. The property was owned by an accountant and had been renovated fifteen years ago. The units were small but modern. The kitchens and baths had updated fixtures and each apartment had central air conditioning which is a big plus in this town (most people who rent are accustomed to window air conditioning units). A few of the apartments were vacant but I felt that I could have them ready quickly and the building 100% leased for a gross rent of $3,600 a month. We agreed on a price of $200,000 with the seller to hold a $30,000 mortgage. Even though we had ample access to cash, the old axiom of using OPM (Other People's Money) should always be attempted under certain market conditions. Considering this was the year 2000 and still a buyer's market, I was comfortable the seller would accept. Within a month we closed on the deal and sure enough the vacant apartments rented without much headache.

How would I define 'without much headache'? Well, after we bought the building someone broke the glass out of a window on the vacant first floor apartment. We also had a noxious odor develop over the course of a few weeks in the common area hallway. At first I checked the basement but everything appeared okay. After several more days the smell grew more intense so I went into the basement again. Due to the odd configuration and numerous walls I had failed to see a crack in the sewer line and raw sewage pooling in a back room. Did I panic? Did we throw up our hands & sell the building? Of course not. Like I've stated before, if you're going to be in this or any business you've got to be prepared for all the hurdles that stand in your way to success.

I had the glass repaired and bars added to the outside of the window. As for the sewage, one phone call to ServiceMaster and the problem was solved. Within several hours they had two guys pumping that mess into a tank and the affected flooring treated with antibiotic chemicals. Not every moment of the day was spent wheeling & dealing and creating a fortune. I simply resolved these minor hiccups and kept plowing ahead.

'If there were never any clouds, how could we ever appreciate the sun'
-Anonymous

While waiting to close on the 8 unit building, I was moving ahead with offers on two other properties. Everything I found was in the same neighborhood as most of my other buildings & all were within walking distance of each other. Around the corner from where we'd purchased the auction property was 2502 N. Calvert Street. This was a nice 3 unit building in need of remodeling with small but well laid out apartments. We grabbed this little gem for $45,000 cash and with a little work had it fully rented for $1,900 a month. One thing I learned from the auction property was to not waste money installing brand new heat only systems instead of a complete unit equipped with air conditioning. Installing heat only will save a little money up front, but having apartments in older buildings with central air is a huge selling point. I made sure in this new project to budget for central air which included having to install all new ductwork. It cost us a little over $10,000 to do all 3 units, but the return on investment was well worth it.

The next property was just a few blocks further up the same street at 2843 N. Calvert. This was a big four unit building that had been well maintained by the current owner. The property had been in his family for a long time and he was ready to liquidate some of his portfolio. Unlike the other buildings Red Sculpture had been buying, this one had separate meters for gas & electric but the heat for the entire building was supplied by one boiler and included in the rent.

The gross monthly rents totaled just over $2,800. Since the building had been owned by the family for generations I guessed that the seller had plenty of equity. I decided to offer a purchase price of $120,000 with $40,000 paid in cash at settlement and the seller to hold a note for the $80,000 balance payable in ten years at 8% interest. He accepted my initial offer and within thirty days we closed the deal. Within just a few short months Red Sculpture had 19 apartments spread across 4 buildings.

I was delighted a few weeks after we closed when the seller called to say he had a similar building in the same neighborhood. It was not quite as large and the rents were slightly less, but I knew a great deal when I saw it and offered the same price and terms. He readily agreed and we quickly picked up another building. Both of these buildings needed absolutely no work and came fully rented. As work progressed on our renovations I continued my pursuit.

Again in the same neighborhood I came across a shell in need of complete rehabilitation. Located at 2427 N. Calvert, it was a massive single family townhouse with 3 floors and an open floor plan. We envisioned the completed project as sleek and hip with a cool metallic urban feel. It was listed for $20,000. Now, keeping in mind that the place was completely gutted down to the brick and needed to be re-built with everything new, I called the listing agent and told him the best I could offer was $5,000.

I had never heard anyone verbally express their utter disdain and disbelief as this agent did. Sputtering and stammering, he let it be known that my offer was outrageous. I reminded him that he was obligated to present any offer to his client no matter what he thought of it personally. The following morning he called with a counter offer of $7,000. Unless a market is sizzling hot, like the 2002 through 2005 cycle, you should never assume what another party will accept. You've got to be bold and ask. The absolute worst that could happen is they will say no.

CHAPTER 13

Where art thou market….

By now it was early 2001 and Red Sculpture was in full swing. Any vacancies that required minimal work were quickly turned over and rented. The renovation work was proceeding well at 2427 Saint Paul and 2502 N. Calvert. Now that we had 6 buildings and a total of 27 units, Andrew thought it best to open an office to handle the property management. Due to its great central location and the fact that we owned it, the small office on the first floor of 2427 Saint Paul was a perfect site.

I quickly hired a receptionist and got the tiny office squared away with the basics; 2 phones, 2 computers, 2 desks, a file cabinet and a fax/copier. All of the furniture and even the copier were 'donated' by Boxer Property. A few months earlier I had evicted a couple of attorneys for non-payment of rent and had held on to their abandoned office furniture. Within a very short time and with little expense Red Sculpture Property Management was up and running.

It was difficult to know it at the time, but Red Sculpture was about to hit the wall. Most economists now agree that the heady stock market of the 1990's ended around March of 2000. Just as we were revving up on our real estate domination of the Baltimore market, millions of stock investors were pulling their shrunken gains out of that market and turning to real estate. Up until this time the stock investors had snubbed their noses at real estate as the tech & bio industries soared. Now that cooler heads, and old fashioned common sense, made mince meat of the stock market, suddenly leaking toilets and whining tenants didn't seem so bad. In fact, many of these investors reasoned that if they could get just a meager 5 to 8% return they would be ahead of the game. After all, even a minuscule gain would be preferred over the massive losses that many had just suffered in their 401(k)'s.

The real estate market, for me locally as well as the entire country, was about to be catapulted to stardom. The market that I had grown accustomed to for the last four years was abruptly ending and so with it went the Red Sculpture dreams.

'It is not enough to know how to ride, you must also know how to fall'
-Mexican proverb

Throughout 2001, I searched diligently for more deals but found nothing appropriately priced. Prices were beginning to swell and the numbers just didn't work. I will explain in detail the simple formula I use to arrive at my purchase price, but it didn't take a math whiz to know that the market was moving dramatically. A building with gross monthly rents of $1,500 that a year ago had an asking price of 115k was now on the market for 175k. Without the rents rising as fast as the prices, it didn't take long for the few remaining good deals to be snatched up. If only we had known that the property values were going to continue to spiral upwards we would've acted accordingly. Instead of relying on cash flow formulas to ensure a good deal, we simply would have bought based on location and waited for the appreciation over the next few years.

Hindsight is always 20/20. It was mid-2001 and the buyers market I had enjoyed was now the size of a pinhead. Around this time I was beginning to feel burned out with all of the real estate. In addition to everything we were doing with Red Sculpture, I still had 70 apartments of my own that had to be managed and maintained. By the fall of 2001 with nothing progressing on the Red Sculpture purchases, Andrew decided it was best to sell off the portfolio and extricate ourselves from this venture. While this was probably little more than a pet project for him, I began to think a lot about leaving real estate for good.

Even though I have a real estate license & could've acted as our own agent to save on the commission, I brought in a real estate broker that I had worked with in the past. Ben Frederick Realty is well known in the Baltimore area and specializes in only commercial & investment property. I was confident that his knowledge & experience would more than offset the additional costs of using an agent. Sure enough, within a short while we had all of the Red Sculpture properties under contract with a partnership from California.

By April 2002 Red Sculpture Properties was done. The buyers had asked us to hold 2nd mortgages on all the houses, so even though the properties were sold it would be awhile until I saw any money.

In fact, it wasn't until about a year later when the new owners did a refinance and paid us off that I received any money. I think my total profit was between $15,000 and $20,000 after two years of work. I know that I didn't have to put up a dime of my own money, but this was a heck of a lot less than I had anticipated when we started. I also did not receive any salary/compensation for managing the properties, dealing with tenants, maintenance, etc.

Andrew nailed it when he referred to Red Sculpture as 'a fortunate failure'. We had not lost any money, but it was a far cry from what we had hoped to be a huge success.

CHAPTER 14

The Great Mistake….

With the wind knocked out of my sails from the Red Sculpture deal & the never ending craziness of dealing with my own 70 apartments, I decided to get out of real estate altogether. I had spent years building up my little empire of properties and had carefully analyzed the numbers before each purchase. I had negotiated favorable prices & terms when buying each building. I had done whatever it took to get each one financed. A few years earlier I had envisioned all of these properties as my retirement nest egg with all the mortgages paid and a large monthly income from all the rent payments. I had spent all this time building something from scratch and then in a flash I decided to sell it all.

I thought I would be much happier with a 'regular' business; something that had 9 to 5 hours of operation, sold some type of product, had an office & a few employees. I glistened at the thought of having some type of business that wouldn't call me at night about a leaking toilet.

"The true way to render ourselves happy is to love our work and find in it our pleasure"
-Francoise De Motteville

One lovely spring morning in 2002 thousands of Baltimore residents awakened to the sight of dozens of For Sale signs lining the sidewalks of Saint Paul & Calvert streets. In one fell swoop I had flooded the market with numerous multi-unit apartment buildings. As the real estate market began to heat up I had full price offers & most of my buildings under contract within a month.

I began to read the local monthly Business Opportunity paper to sift through ideas for my next venture. One particular ad for a medical supply company caught my eye so I began to investigate it in earnest.

I called the broker & received financial statements on the business. It was tucked in an off street business park north of Washington DC and had a small office, warehouse & five employees. Despite the fact that the owner rarely made an appearance, the owner's daughter worked there part time and according to the financials it made a decent profit each year.

I thought this was a good business to enter because:

- the baby boomer market was enormous & the need for medical attention is exploding
- I was told the employees had a lot of experience
- I could relocate to a retail center to attract more business
- They had no decent advertising in the Yellow Pages. I thought a larger & more detailed ad would equal more sales
- Insurance companies paid for many of the products
- They had no web site & therefore I could start an online store to add business
- The business had a lot of accounts receivable money on the books & I assumed a more hands-on owner would be able to collect some of it

With a $100,000 small business administration loan, $123,000 financed by the owner and $20,000 loaned by my credit union I threw myself into this new adventure.

Within 36 hours of buying this business, I knew I had made the biggest mistake of my life. (at the end of this chapter I'll give you an expanded list of every dumb thing I did during this debacle so that hopefully you will learn from me & not make the same mistakes).

My second morning at the office I asked the employees about the company's biggest customer; a large, upscale nursing home in the suburbs of Washington D.C. Imagine the look on my face when they said, 'Didn't the previous owner tell you? They're no longer a customer of ours'. This customer represented about 20% of the business with large consistent purchases every month. Knowing he was about to sell, the previous owner had squeezed them to pay all of their bills before I took over. At the same time, he instructed the employees not to make any deliveries to them unless absolutely necessary. After a month of this treatment the nursing home got fed up & started making some calls. They discovered that they could buy most of what they needed directly from the manufacturer and completely cut us out of the picture.

Again with 20/20 hindsight, I should've stopped right there and called the SBA lender to put a stop on that $100,000 check. I would've cut my losses (about $10k in attorney fees to handle the closing, etc.) and gotten the hell out of there.

I guess since I was able to purchase millions of dollars of real estate starting with nothing, I thought I could get this mess straightened out & turn it around.

"The eye sees only what the mind is prepared to comprehend"
-Henri Bergson

From day one I suffered a negative cash flow in the medical supply business and it never got better. Every two weeks I had to deposit $6,000 to $10,000 just to meet payroll and pay bills. And where was this money coming from? The money used to keep the medical supply afloat was the profit from the sale of my apartment buildings.

Throughout 2002 and into 2003 I continued to try and market this new business & make it profitable. I expanded our Yellow Pages ad, attended trade shows, cold called nursing homes & doctor's offices. I hired a full time salesperson to try and kick up the dust. The previous owner had outsourced the medical billing to the insurance companies. I decided to hire a full time person to do our own billing internally as I assumed this would give us more control of how & when we billed the insurance.

None of this worked. And all of this ate away at my real estate nest egg which initially totaled almost $660,000 in cash!

I only made a few wise decisions during this period of my life:

- I used a chunk of the money to put a large down payment on a great house in a golf course community in Ellicott City, MD.
- I refused to pay the previous owner any of the $123,000 note that he held due to his mishandling of the company while it was under contract of sale. After some legal wrangling back & forth, I agreed to pay him $15,000 cash.

By the spring of 2004 it was all over. The landlord had filed for an eviction of the office and warehouse space. The power company had turned off the electricity and I held a going out of business sale to get whatever cash I could for the inventory. Of course, none of the employees were surprised when I let them go. They knew the end was near when a month earlier I stopped depositing money into the company bank account.

After all the smoke cleared and the dust settled, I was left with a nice house (with a mortgage), a personally guaranteed SBA loan with a $100,000 balance and I owed over $100,000 in income taxes from the sale of my properties.

I had no rental property income whatsoever. The medical supply nightmare had swallowed all of my cash. I had no job, no prospect of where to turn next and no idea how I was going to support my family.

After coming so far, only to crash & burn like this left me emotionally and mentally devastated. I was 34 years old and had allowed a small self-made fortune to slip through my fingers. I still get a knot in my stomach whenever I think about it.

I know all the rah-rah self confidence talk. I know that we learn from our failures and that by learning we will be more successful in the future. I know that our mistakes are supposed to have a positive effect by teaching & guiding us. But this was one hell of a life lesson!

"It requires a great deal of boldness and a great deal of caution to make a great fortune; and when you have got it, it requires ten times s much wit to keep it"
-Meyer Rothschild

If I were to envision the ideal business, it would probably look something like this:

- I would have confident knowledge of the industry
- Located at home or within 15 minutes from home
- No debt or personal guarantees
- No employees (or at least only have exceptional employees)
- No billing or accounts receivable- only accept cash or credit card up front
- No inventory to store & maintain

Now let's examine how the medical supply business I bought compares to the ideal business:

- I didn't really know a thing about medical supplies. I worked for a while as a delivery driver for a medical supply company (delivering to people's homes, set up temporary electric beds in their rooms, etc). I think that hardly qualifies as having a commanding knowledge of the industry and taking control of such a business.
- It took me 45 to 60 minutes (one way) to get to the office.
- I not only personally guaranteed a large SBA loan, I also personally signed for the Yellow Pages advertising, the credit card equipment and lines of credit with most of the vendors. About the only thing I didn't personally guaranty

was the rent for the office. When we were evicted it was filed against the company & there were no personal guarantees in the lease.

- Most of the employees tried to do a good job, but like most people they were not result oriented. My pep talks & motivational speeches created a small blip of productivity, but it was always short-lived.

- Our payments from the insurance companies and Medicare were abysmal. On a typical $100 sale they would only pay us about $60. Then they would state that we couldn't collect the full balance from the patient, so in the end we would receive a total of about $65 on a $100 sale. In most instances the $65 was barely enough to cover the cost of inventory, let alone payroll, rent, etc. It was a flawed reimbursement cycle and I should have educated myself much better before being consumed by it.

Probably the single greatest mistake I made was not seeking out wise counsel before I made this purchase. A good business consultant would've spotted most of the potholes in this company & steered me away from it. If only I had taken a crowbar and pried open my wallet for about a thousand bucks, all this heartache could've been avoided.

If you remember nothing else, remember these last few pages. Don't ever substitute confidence for true knowledge on a subject. There's no shame in seeking out help & assistance from an impartial third party. It'll be the smartest money you'll ever invest. Not only could it help you make a fortune, but as in my case, it could keep you from losing a fortune.

CHAPTER 15

The real estate market was sizzling hot in 2004 but I was gun shy about jumping back in. The numbers still didn't justify buying property to hold as a rental (especially since the prices were getting so high that the rents could never support a positive cash flow). The idea of buying with the *hope* of profiting through quick appreciation also didn't entice me. All I could picture was overpaying just before the music stopped and every investor scrambled for a chair!

To get some money flowing into my pocket, I made a quick decision to start a contracting business to help all the new investors entering the market. We would do renovation work on rehab projects and offer maintenance service for rental property.

I purchased a white contractors van, hired a few handymen and began contacting old acquaintances (landlords I knew, property management companies, other people that I had done business with when I had my apartments, etc). Within a few months my little quick start operation had 5 full time employees and $106,000 in sales.

But I wasn't happy. I was constantly running all over Baltimore giving estimates and looking at projects. Many people were just shopping for the best price and wasting my time with unreasonable expectations. If all I wanted was to put a few bucks in my pocket each day, then maybe I would've had more of my estimates accepted. But I was trying to run a business with the purpose of making a consistent profit margin.

Another thing that drove me away from doing contracting work for others was the fact that the vast majority of these investors had not a clue of what they were doing- but they were making money anyway! This drove me nuts.

How could someone pay, what I considered, entirely too much for a property? Then use the wrong materials (high quality fixtures in a low/middle income rental neighborhood). Then have work done in the wrong order (painting walls first, then doing plumbing/electrical later which usually resulted in damage to the floors & walls). Then they would rent to the worse tenants & not have a clue how to evict them. Then they would sell the property a year later and almost double their money. It suddenly hit me like a lightning bolt to the forehead that if these people were stumbling all over themselves & still making money, then I should get back to my roots and start buying again.

And that's exactly what I did.

CHAPTER 16

"There isn't much thrill in success unless one has first been close to failure"
-William Feather

Since late 2004 to the present, I have been focused on buying, renovating & selling vacant property in Baltimore. I use private lenders to fund the purchase and repair costs. I kept my best crew from my contracting business and use them full time to do 80% of the renovations. The roof, windows and HVAC work is done by sub-contractors (my crew could do all of it, but then I wouldn't be able to churn 5 to 10 projects month after month).

Despite the current cooling of the seller's market and the collapse of the sub-prime market (lenders who give loans at high interest rates to homeowners with bad credit), I am bullish on real estate. Of course, I don't mean 'bullish' as in the frenzied haphazard buying of the last few years. I simply mean that I am upbeat and positive of the market. As of August 2007, interest rates are still at historic lows which is great for investors. The more people that can genuinely afford what I have to sell means more opportunity for me.

But prices in most areas are still a little too high, therefore a prudent approach is to always hunt for bargains. Rarely will you lose money when you buy at the right price. Unfortunately, so many new investors inflated the market over the last few years that a shake up is inevitable.

Unlike the dot com bubble, I think real estate will continue to have a soft landing in most parts of the country. There is inherent value in land and buildings- you simply can't create any more land so the value will never go to zero.

Back in the late nineties, cocktail party conversation invariably centered around the stock or IPO of the moment. I saw that as the death rattle of the market; as soon as something becomes popular and the masses jump on, it's over.

In 2005, I felt the same way about real estate. Everyone knew someone who was flipping or rehabbing. The residential homeowner market was already hot, but the investment property market really didn't explode until 2004. I remember seeing my doctor and being peppered with questions about investing in real estate. I've kept my guard up ever since; I hunt carefully for the best deals I can find so that I don't get burned.

As of August 2007, I am focused on small single unit vacant rental property that I can fix-up and sell to investors. Surprisingly, many real estate investors prefer not to buy properties that need a lot of renovation work. Instead, they're looking for a turnkey rental where someone else has already done all the hard work and the house only needs to be rented & maintained.

This is where I come in. Right now, I am that 'someone' doing all the renovation work. I purchase houses quickly using my private lenders, do the repairs as expeditiously as possible without taking shortcuts on quality and then sell the finished house to an investor who will hold it for a long term rental.

I prefer to get in and out quickly, make $15,000 to $25,000 profit per deal, and do as many houses as I can each month. As the market continues to soften I may start holding some properties as long term rentals, but right now I'm enjoying making money as fast as I can!

BONUS CHAPTERS

The purpose of these bonus sections is to give you some highlights of what has worked well for me in the past. There have been volumes written on every aspect of real estate from raising capital to selling your projects yourself and everything in between.

If you're serious about investing in real estate or any other business endeavor, I strongly encourage reading everything you can about the subject. I've probably read over 500 books on real estate, business, management, self-help and biographies of successful people. To be honest, most them weren't very good. But if I learned just one or two things by reading a whole book, listening to a tape or attending a seminar then it was worth the effort. My attempt now is to quickly condense the best of what I've personally used so that you can get started as fast as possible.

Another good thing about the current real estate market is that many of the novices have either become smarter about their purchases or have been flushed completely out of the market. In general, from buyers & sellers to agents and lenders, a sense of realism has finally pierced the euphoria of the market and allowed cooler heads to prevail.

BONUS #1 FIND IT, FIX IT, SELL IT

This is the strategy I'm currently using because the numbers work right now. As the market changes I will look again to buying small apartment buildings and holding onto them.

FIND IT

I use a variety of methods to find potential deals. I've bought property using MLS real estate listings, bank & lender REO's, estate sales, short sales and auctions. My best deals, however, have always come from my letters (sample at end of book). The best time to get a great deal is when no else knows about it. That's why I've always been a huge fan of direct mail letters.

You can use a mailing list and/or a direct mail company to send letters to every absentee owner for an entire zip code, stuff & mail them yourself to a few select streets/neighborhoods, or use them whenever you drive by a house that your interested in. It used to be a lot easier for me to get deals with my letters before the market went crazy, but I still get calls & nice comments all the time. My letter is sincere, honest and up front. You can tweak it to fit your own personal style. I always print it on cream colored paper rather than plain white and I always stamp the envelope with my name & home address.

Think about it. Which would prompt you to call me? Something that was printed crooked on a postcard with a company name & PO Box as the return address or a nice letter clearly written and signed by a real person?

Some sellers get bombarded with mailings all the time. You want your mailing piece to stand just a little taller than the crowd. Spending just a little more time and money will make a big difference.

I know that many real estate gurus say to let the world know you're an investor; hand out tons of cards, put a magnetic sign on the side of your car, etc. I prefer to operate quietly under the surface and target property no one else is trying to buy.

What to pay?

There's no substitute for knowing your market when it comes to property valuation. Looking at a deal through rose-colored glasses will almost always get you in trouble. The only thing that spared novice investors over the last few years from getting burned was the dramatic appreciation of property values across the country. No offense, but two years ago a monkey could've bought a house and figured out how to turn a profit on it. Now that things have cooled, your best bet is to research, research, research.

Developing a relationship with a good agent is absolutely necessary if you lack knowledge of the market. You should also research private sales that wouldn't show up on the MLS. Many searches are now available for free online. Try Googling 'Real Property Data (plus your city/area)' to research private sales in your area.

To stay out of trouble, I recommend the following formula:

ARV (after repair value) X 70% - repair costs = Total Offer Price
Example:
$125,000 (ARV) X 70% = $87,500
$87,500 - $15,000 (repairs) = $72,500 (maximum offer price)

Therefore, my offer price on this deal should be no more than $72,500. Depending on your particular market/street/neighborhood and the overall condition of the property you may want to lower or raise your offer accordingly. Typically, I would offer something lower, say 65% or $66,250 just to give myself a little cushion.

Part of the reason I like to use 65% in my buying formula is to help cover the additional costs I'll incur when selling. Maryland has some of the highest closing costs in the nation. I usually factor an expense of 8.5% of the selling price of my fixed up property- 6% for the agent commission and 2.5% for closing costs in Baltimore. On our $125,000 example this equates to $10,625 just in closing costs! Yet another reason for making sure you buy at a low price or don't buy it at all.

Key Point

When buying property with the intention of reselling it soon, I always write my offers with no contingencies; no financing contingencies, no inspections, no 'weasel' clauses so that I can get out of the deal.

If you're assigning contracts or doing some other type of flip & not actually taking title and buying the property, then this strategy probably won't work. You'll want some kind of weasel clause in case you can't find someone to assign your contract to.

Some people negotiate a price & then use the inspections, appraisal, etc. to beat up on the seller and get a lower price or get a discount for the repairs.

My strategy is to hit them with a very low price right up front, but then promise an easy and stress-free settlement for them. I'll buy their house 'as-is' with absolutely no hassles and settle within 30 days. This usually gets me better deals with a lot less headache.

Buy really low. Pay cash (more on this later). After they agree to your price, don't nickel & dime the seller.

FIX IT

I could write about this until my fingers bleed. There are no real secrets or tips here. You've got to get your feet wet and learn.

By far, the number #1 reason people lose money (besides paying to much for the property) is by being wholly unrealistic on the repair budget.

Think about it. Most deals are vacant, beat up and abandoned property that was probably poorly maintained even when it used to be occupied. And yet, many investors will have such extremely tight budgets that it only takes a few slight variables to throw their profit out the window.

In fact, most investors plan their budget <u>based on the amount of funds they have available</u> for a particular project, *instead of what's <u>realistically needed to be done to the property to make it sell</u>!*

This is backwards! Before you buy a house you've got to be realistic about the costs and plan accordingly.

Contractors

When hiring contractors it's best to get references. I typically only use a contractor that someone else has recommended. This has the added effect of them knowing that if they screw around with my job it may affect the relationship they have with the person who gave the recommendation.

Cheaper rarely means better. There are times when I'm working on a rental property that I'll fix up & re-sell where I don't want to put the best labor & materials into it. The painting & cosmetics don't have to be the same standard as a homeowner rehab. If I'm uncomfortable with a 'cheap' contractor and I'm having, for example, windows or carpentry work done, then I'll pay for the material directly and only pay them after the work is completed.

This won't keep you from getting burned, but it will lessen the odds. We all get burned sometimes. I recently did for $500 on a window job. All you can do is learn and keep pushing forward.

SELL IT

This one is easy- use a good real estate agent to sell your fixed up houses. Period.

Although I have a license and could act as my own agent to save money on the commission, in the long run I wouldn't save anything & probably would end up spending more money. Why?

Because as I've grown and gotten a little wiser I've come to one conclusion that I know to be true- I stink at selling houses. I don't have the time to constantly do showings, I don't like dealing directly with homebuyers and it would take me longer to find a qualified buyer because I'm not a full-time agent, so therefore I just don't do it. If you're an investor, the only reason (and it's a good one) to have a real estate license is to make you a better buyer (quick access to MLS, firm understanding of contact law, etc).

Also, don't be afraid to ask your agent or others for constructive criticism on your properties. You may have overlooked things that would help the sale like sprucing up the landscaping or replacing the old front porch light. The better agents I know tell their clients up front what will help make the house sell faster. You may not act on every suggestion, but at least you'll have a feel for how others look at the house & what you might do differently in the future (Ex. expanding the size of a bathroom or not expanding it because it wouldn't really have increased the sales price).

BONUS #2 LANDLORD 101

Part 1

Buying rental property is how I lifted myself out of obscurity and allowed my wife to be a stay-at-home mom. I've owned everything from single family houses to small apartment buildings and there are pro's & con's to each.

The biggest benefit of single family houses (whether detached or a rowhouse) is that the tenant pays 100% of the utilities. There can be no question as to who is responsible when the water bill comes in high or the electric bill is spiraling in the winter. And if they don't pay it, they're the ones left without power. It doesn't affect you.

The major downside to single's is if you have too many turnovers. A multi-unit should be able to absorb a vacancy without much trouble. But with a single unit your income is zero when it's vacant. Worse, if you have to paint, carpet or do any major repairs because of bad tenants you could easily eat up a year's worth of profit getting it in move-in condition for the next tenant.

I prefer multi-units over single family houses for a variety of reasons. Most important is the cash flow. If the building is bought for the right price, multi-units can throw a good profit month after month.

They're also a lot easier to maintain. Think about it- would you rather have 20 houses scattered throughout the city or one 20 unit building in a decent part of town?

Establish the right purchase price & stay out of trouble

When you're buying & flipping houses and not planning on holding it long term then the appraised value is very important. But when I'm buying rental property, I really don't care what the appraised value happens to be. Even though the building should appreciate over time & create more equity (money) for me, I like to focus solely on the cash flow when buying. Regardless of what method you prefer, the numbers have to work.

Some people take the total rent and divide it by 1% to arrive at a price.
Ex. Monthly rents are $1,500 / 1% = $150,000 purchase price.

I don't use this formula! It doesn't take into account the expenses of owning a rental. It's a quick rule of thumb value, at best.

The formula that I prefer is the capitalization rate. The cap rate formula has many applications, especially for commercial & large scale projects, but I find it very useful for valuing small rentals. The cap rate is simply the net operating income (NOI) divided by the purchase price.

Ex. $8,000 (NOI) / $100,000 (purchase price) = 8.0% cap rate

Ex. $8,000 (NOI) / $80,000 (purchase price) = 10.0 % cap rate

Notice how the <u>lower</u> the price goes, the <u>higher</u> the cap rate. When buying, you want a high cap rate.

Now lets discuss a few things that people tend to do to completely muck up this simple formula. Namely, they don't calculate the net operating income correctly, they try to factor in a down payment, and worst of all they settle for too low a cap rate when buying.

Calculating Net Operating Income

Whether it's a single house rental or a 50 unit building, calculating the NOI correctly is critical. These expenses <u>must</u> be taken into account: vacancy rate, advertising, insurance, property taxes, maintenance, property management, licenses/registration and utilities.

A typical 3 unit building in a decent section of Baltimore might have numbers that look like this:

Gross Rent (annual)	27,000	
Vacancy Loss (5%)	1,350	
Advertising	150	$50 per unit
Insurance	1,200	$400 per unit
Maintenance	1,500	$500 per unit
Property Tax	1,600	
Property Management	1,800	
License/Registration	150	$50 per unit
Electric & Gas	500	
Water	1,500	$500 per unit
Net Operating Income	**$17,250**	

Now comes the important part- what is an acceptable cap rate? Some people like to factor in a down payment & their loan when creating a cap rate. I never do. I treat the cap rate just like a return on investment (ROI) in the stock market. If XYZ stock has an annual return of 9% (cap rate) and I purchase $100,000 worth of shares in cash, then my ROI would be $9,000 (let's not get too mired in the details like margin accounts, expenses, etc).

In the example above there is a $17,250 net operating income (also referred to as 'net before debt'). If I wanted an 11% return on my investment, then I would pay no more than $156,818 for this property. It doesn't matter if I'm paying all cash, financing 100% with a lender or any other combination of loans, I still measure my return based on the net operating income. If the property experiences terrific appreciation then that's icing on the cake, but by basing my purchase price solely on the income & expenses of the building it greatly reduces my risk.

I never bought any rental property with a rate less than 15%. Rarely will you find deals with this rate of return if the building is completely renovated & fully rented. The owners probably put money into the building to get it in good condition and are not going to sell on the cheap. But, you never know unless you ask. If you make offers using my formula, your odds of succeeding go up dramatically. Plus, by using my formula you'll quickly know a good deal when you find it!

Using at least 15% also creates a healthy spread if you use 100% financing. If you're getting a 15% ROI and your mortgage has an interest rate of 7%, your effective return is now an 8% profit. When you buy property, like many do, with a cap rate of 9% and your mortgage loan has an interest rate of 7%, your effective return is now just 2%. This is not a good enough cushion. At that low of a cap rate, you're working harder for the bank to pay off the loan than for yourself.

Remember my story & all those great deals? They had cap rates from 15% to 30%! And where did I find many of the deals?

1. Frustrated Landlords who wanted out.
2. Properties that needed a few cosmetic repairs.
3. Poorly managed properties.

Most cities have a public listing of rent evictions. By doing a little leg work you could mail a letter to all of the property owners who file evictions month after month. I'm sure you'll find a few frustrated landlords ready to make a deal.

Remember one of those 7 unit buildings I bought that had a property management company taking care of the building for the owner? Well they took care of him all right. On his financial statement the owner was paying hundreds of dollars a year on locks. As soon as I saw that, I was certain many of the other numbers were padded as well. Without immediately raising rents, I had a $1,000 per month positive cash flow just by eliminating all of the garbage this poor guy was being overcharged!

Always remember that when buying a rental property for the long term the appraised value is important to know, but getting the cap rate at 15% or higher is what will make you money.

BONUS #3 LANDLORD 101

Part 2

We've looked at what to buy & how to price it. Now we're ready to discuss the most dreaded word in the landlord's vocabulary-Tenants.

I honestly don't remember where I heard it or who even said it, but the absolute best advice I can give you on renting to tenants is this:

The #1 Rule: Having your unit vacant is better than having a Bad Tenant

No truer words have ever been spoken. Believe me, I've been there.

It's late at night. I can't sleep. I've got 100 apartments and a $14,000 mortgage payment due on the first. Five of the units are vacant, another eight are slow to pay and I've got three units going to rent court. Not long ago, this was a typical month for me.

The urge becomes overwhelming to just start throwing warm bodies, <u>any</u> bodies, into the vacant units to get some cash flow. You think you'll be able to manage them, correct them, show them the previous erring of their ways and magically only for you they'll pay their rent on the 1st of every month. They love the apartment & solemnly promise to pay. They talk about the new job they're starting next week & that money will be no problem.

I've heard it all. Rather than bore you with volumes of 'war stories' about all that went wrong, let me give you my quick tips on true landlording that hopefully will keep you ahead of the curve. If you haven't figured out by now, I'm a big believer in having simple systems/formulas for everything I do. Once I find something that works I stick to it. By no means did I learn all of this overnight. What you are about to learn took me <u>years</u> of trial & error. If your goal is to own 5 apartments in the next few years or 500, I can show you the way. My tenants educated me like no college ever could.

Finding Tenants

Finding good tenants starts with having a good place to rent to them. Even in a bad part of town, no decent person is going to live in a bad place (at least not for very long). When I was doing contracting work for other property owners I did some business for this one company that owned a couple of hundred apartments in a so-so part of Baltimore. They would vacate/evict the tenant on Monday & have the unit turned over and ready for a new tenant to move in by that weekend. On the phone I marveled at their efficiency & imagined what great systems they must have in place to keep their operation running so smoothly.

I soon discovered how smooth they really were. The apartment I committed to get ready for them was absolutely disgusting. I wouldn't let my dog spend the night in there let alone someone's family. There was mold on the walls and the bathroom was filthy. The only work I agreed to do was replace the kitchen countertop, replace a few broken doors and some other light punch-out work. By Friday they had their painter come in and spray a thick coat of cheap paint right over the mold & grime.

That was the only job I did for those people. They were truly slumlords and I wanted no part of that shoddy business.

I never show a vacant apartment to a prospective tenant until it has been painted & cleaned. Don't show a rundown unit to someone & then tell them how you're going to fix it up. Always do the work first, make it presentable, and then bring them in. You can't expect a tenant to have a 'vision' of what the place will look like after it's fixed up. Remember, the crummy tenants will take anything. I once had a girl tell me over the phone that she needed a place immediately & she didn't care if there were holes in the walls or if the apartment was a total wreck. I politely told her I couldn't help her and hung up the phone. What kind of renter do you think she would've been? Always paying on time? No problems? I would've gotten a security deposit and first month's rent and then be fighting to get her out.

Good places attract good tenants. Bad places attract bad tenants. It's pretty simple.

If you ever purchase a multi-unit building with a few bad tenants you should work to get them out as soon as possible. I call it re-tenanting a building. You cycle out the bad and bring in the good. Your good tenants won't put up with crazy behavior and late night loudness; they'll simply move out without notice one weekend and leave you scratching your head. Better to be proactive & let your good tenants know your on top of the situation rather than let them slip away.

So you've got a decent place & it's ready to be rented. You didn't go overboard on expensive countertops and imported ceramic tile. It's clean, sanitary and presentable. You could give the keys to someone & they could move in that night.

So now you're ready to put a For Rent sign in the window, right?

Wrong.

Okay, how about a long-winded ad in the paper with your phone number in big letters so you get lots of calls?

Wrong again.

I've used both of these marketing techniques and they stink. All you get is your voicemail filled with tire-kickers wanting more information. Ever try returning 45 phone calls after dinner? But wait, it gets even more fun because after you've returned all those calls you now have a dozen or so that want to see the apartment. So now you're juggling your schedule and running over to the property at different times to show the unit. And the best part- half of the time they don't even show up. They don't even call you on your cell to say they're not coming.

Out of frustration I came up with a rarely used technique to show an apartment according to my schedule. I put an ad in the Sunday edition of the paper under the Real Estate for Rent section like this:

Open House!

Baltimore- 618 Waverly St. Open

Tuesday 7/3 @ 5:00pm. Nice 2 BD,

1 BA. $650/month + sec. dep.

Notice that there's no phone number. Notice that I didn't put between 5:00 and 7:00pm. You can add more of a description, but I like to keep it simple & clean. I used to use Monday @ 5:00pm but I found that many people don't get around to actually reading their Sunday paper until Monday. So doing it Tuesday gives them a little extra time to re-arrange their schedule so that they can make it.

I've used this ad hundreds of times and it works. I might have to do an open house a few weeks in a row, but it still beats the heck out of all that wasted time on the phone. Also, this ad helps weed out all of the tire-kickers! If someone is serious about renting a place, they will come to the open house on time and be anxious to get it. I usually get less than a dozen people at my open houses. Some walk through quickly and leave, some ask a few questions and leave, and a few more ask for an application and fill it out on the spot.

Using this technique will save you a ton of headaches. You don't want volume. You want quality. Having 90 people respond to your sign & ad with phone calls may sound great to a novice, but I'd much rather spend a half hour of my time with a targeted gathering of prospective tenants. An added benefit when you acquire more buildings is that you can direct someone to the right place for them. They may not like the apartment your showing right now, but the apartment being vacated in another building at the end of the month may be perfect for them.

As any good salesman will tell you, it's all about getting qualified leads. I've rented apartments a week before Christmas & remember people telling me beforehand that nobody would show up. If you have a decent place, they will come. There will always be exceptions; bad weather, lull in the rental market, etc. But in good parts of town and bad, this advertising system has proven itself. It works.

Qualifying Tenants

This can be a little tricky. I used to do full applications and a credit check. I won't dissuade you from doing this, but I've been burned by people with good credit plenty of times.

The most important qualifier I use is a good conversation. While someone is walking through my open house, I use that time wisely. I make light conversation peppered with questions on why they're moving, what they do for a living, how long have they done it and do they have any friends or family nearby. They think I'm just being friendly.

I am, but I'm also probing. An application is too sterile for me. I like to hear their voice and see their body language when they answer. Knowing why they're moving and how they're going to pay the rent is critical.

I also look for stability. I've never been too crazy about roommates or unmarried couples unless one of them by themselves can afford to cover the rent. If it takes both of their incomes to just get by, then what happens when one of them loses their job? Or they break up? Or the roommates packs up & leaves?

Yup. Their problem just became your problem.

It also doesn't hurt to make a few quick calls and verify some of their information. Most important would be their job. Verify their employment, how long they've been there and how much they make.

Now you're ready to sign the lease, get their deposit & 1st months rent and give them the keys. Never, ever, under any circumstance should you not take a security deposit. And, never allow the tenant to do some sort of improvement in lieu of a deposit, like painting. I once saw beautiful refinished hardwood floors saturated with white paint because some landlord didn't heed this advice. Most people are lousy painters & handyman. Besides, your place shouldn't need any work because you weren't supposed to rent it until it was fixed up, right?

Managing Tenants

I have to tell you that I really don't like using the word tenant or renter. It almost sounds like there is something abhorrent or unsuitable with them. My wife and I have been tenants as well as many of our friends and family. They are not a sub-class of society or to be treated as suspect.

Having said all that, tenants are unique in that they are directly related to your financial, emotional, mental and physical well-being. It would be great if on the 1st of every month you could press a button and all of your rents were direct deposited to your bank account. And for the rest of the month it would be great if there were no maintenance issues and no complaints. Imagine it:

Rent Payment – Mortgage Payment = My Profit

Doesn't that look great? That's how 95% of the people who jump into real estate think. I don't know if you've realized this yet, but you're in the <u>people</u> business, not the real estate business. That building you bought doesn't care who owns it or who lives in it. You <u>will</u> have roof leaks, plumbing leaks, heating malfunctions and general problems associated with the physical aspects of any building. But.....

Your long-term success, or failure, rests solely on how you deal with people.

That's it.

Whether I'm buying a building that's already occupied or signing a lease with a new tenant, I always let them know what's expected of them.

- Rent is due on the first of the month.
- If their payment envelope is postmarked after the 5th, there is a late charge. The post office may be slow to deliver the mail sometimes, but they're pretty good about stamping the date they receive it.
- If no rent is received by the 10th then I file to evict with the rent court.

You'll quickly get a feel for the slow paying tenants & how to deal with them. Some are just chronic late payers and others need an eviction notice before they pay.

Important- Make sure you know the basics of the tenant/landlord laws as it pertains to rent collection & eviction. Each city has different laws and you <u>must</u> know yours. I can assure you that your tenants are aware of them. If you're not, then your tenants may stay one step ahead & frustrate the daylights out of you.

In many areas there are rent court/eviction services that specialize in this procedure. For very little money they will do all the paperwork and go to court on your behalf. They may be a little hard to locate, so your best bet is to find out which courthouse handles evictions in your area <u>and go find out</u>! Don't be lazy. Utilizing their services has been an enormous help to me over the years.

The bottom line is to run your rent collection like a business- it must be completely unemotional. Don't ever let your tenant's problems become <u>your</u> problems.

Treat everyone fairly and the same & you'll stay way ahead of the pack. Don't tell them up front what's expected, let them slide on the rent & then plead for some kind of payment and you will get burned.

I've evicted commercial tenants when I was a property manager for Boxer Property (some of those evicted were attorneys!). I've evicted single mothers with children. I've evicted drug addicts and others down on their luck.

I take no joy in any of it. Personally, it breaks my heart. But if you don't run your rent collection with an iron fist, you will suffer. And if you suffer, so will your family.

One time I was serving out an eviction with a sheriff's deputy (Baltimore law) and a small boy answered the door. He was about ten years old and home alone on a school day! I don't know what became of that family after the eviction or if social services got involved for the child's sake. The place was infested with roaches and huge piles of smelly clothes. It's unthinkable to most of us how anyone could live like that, but they do.

Another time I rented a small apartment to a happy little twenty-something couple and they were literally skipping down the street after I gave them the keys. They were ecstatic and I was happy for them. They were young & in love and renting their first apartment together.

Three months later I was at their apartment, with the sheriff's deputy, serving the eviction. I barely recognized the person who answered the door. It looked like all the drugs she'd consumed had robbed her body of vital nutrients. Her face was pale white with open sores and bloodshot eyes. She was a zombie.

She tried to give me a stained, crumpled personal check to pay for the rent. Before I could open my mouth the deputy told her that only cash could be accepted at this point. He realized how bad they looked as well & knew they had to go. It wasn't until a few hours after the eviction that I realized they'd left their cat behind in the apartment. So on top of everything else, I had to contact animal control and have their cat removed as well.

I'm not trying to bring you down. I don't want to discourage you in the least. I want you to make a ton of money and be wildly successful. It's not all bad; I have plenty of good stories too.

Here's one:

I once rented a rowhouse to a single girl with really bad credit. She had filed bankruptcy earlier that year and no one would rent to her, so she was forced to live with her parents. Because she now had no debt, she was able to save her money. I asked her to pay a security deposit, 1st month's rent and last month's rent. This totaled $2,250 before she even moved in! She stayed for a few years and was one of the best renters I ever had. I assumed, correctly, that since she had no debt she should have no problem paying the rent.

Just be fair, firm and have a plan in place when it comes to getting your money.

Maintenance

Do it. Don't put it off. Besides not wanting to deal with bad neighbors, your good tenants won't deal with an absentee landlord either. A leaky faucet isn't going to magically stop leaking. It will only get worse. Nobody wants to shell out a lot of money for maintenance, but your properties will need attention from time to time. Better to spearhead it and get it done as quickly as possible.

Even if your handyman skills are up to the task, I highly recommend that you hire someone to do the work. Your time will always be better spent elsewhere.

You make more money with your mind than with your hands.

It's also a good idea to open a few accounts with local hardware, lumber & plumbing supply houses. I have two Home Depot accounts, but they don't stock the oddball plumbing & miscellaneous things you come across when repairing property. Although having an account usually doesn't offer any pricing discount, it's extremely productive in that I don't have to run around town getting supplies. Authorized buyers on my crew can go get what they need, put a purchase order on the ticket so I know what property it's for, and keep on rolling.

Utilities

When you're renting a single house to one family the utilities are irrelevant- they pay for all of it. But when you have a multi-unit property, the utilities can quickly become an ugly beast that'll eat right through your profits.

Back in 2000 & 2001 Baltimore Gas & Electric had a slight price hike. We also had an incredibly cold winter snap and when it was all over I was still paying off my heating bills through the next summer. Many of my multi-unit buildings used a single large boiler to heat the entire building. I tried using tamper proof thermostats and kept the temperature set at 70 degrees, but in my larger 7 unit building I would still get bills for over $1,400 a month during the winter.

One day I got the novel idea to eliminate my bill altogether. As tenant leases came up for renewal, or if someone new moved in, I would include in the lease that they pay 1/7th (because there were 7 apartments) of the bill. I would also agree not to raise their rents. Keep in mind that a typical rent increase is 5-10% depending on the area. Instead of increasing someone's rent by say $50, I was able to bill them their percentage of the gas & electric bill for a lot more- typically between $50 and $200 a month! To my surprise, in every building that I tried this not one tenant moved out and no one really complained. People aren't stupid. They know when rates go up for utilities, phone, etc. and they know it's got to be paid somehow.

Within about six months I completely eliminated my utility expense for all of my multi-unit buildings. There are of course a few stipulations. This will only work well in your better buildings with white-collar tenants. If you have a building with a high eviction rate then it's unlikely you're going to get them to pay a separate bill. In those situations it's sometimes best to investigate the costs of having everything separately metered, including the heat. Even if you had to get a small improvement loan, in the long run it may well be worth it.

Another thing that made this successful was utilizing property management software. I found Tenant Pro to be the most flexible at the best price for a small operation. In addition to a host of great features, it allowed me to input my own billing for utilities and keep track of all payments. When I received a monthly bill from BG&E, I would mail a copy of it along with an invoice (produced by Tenant Pro) to each tenant. Giving them a copy of the bill let them know I wasn't trying to make a profit, but that I was simply recovering this expense.

As energy prices continue to soar around the country, this approach may be the way to go instead of just a flat increase in the rent. A final benefit was that the utility bill began to decrease slightly. After the tenants were on the hook for the bill, they began to close windows and become more energy conscious in general. I highly recommend giving it a try.

Water, Water, Everywhere

In addition to slimming the electric, the water bill is something else that must be closely watched. Be proactive and encourage your tenants to tell you when faucets drip or toilets run all day & night. A running toilet in a small 4 unit building that I own recently saddled me with a $2,000 quarterly water bill. After repairing it, the Baltimore water billing department gave me a $1,000 credit, but it was still a lot more than the usual $400 bill.

Whenever one of your maintenance people goes on a call, regardless of why, they should make it a habit to check the toilet & sinks for any problems. They should also keep a few flappers, washers, etc in their vehicle so that a second trip isn't required for a minor repair.

Seventy Five percent of the Earth's surface is covered in water, but only 1% is drinkable. The price of water will continue to go up. Think conservation by using low flow faucet heads & keeping an eye out for leaks, and your wallet will be thanking you later.

The Final Word on Landlording

Just remember to be fair and firm with your tenants. There's no reason to scream and yell. Don't act like you're broke & whine to them about paying you the rent. The lease I use is standard issue, boilerplate copy endorsed by the Greater Baltimore Board of Realtors and several other counties. Keep it simple and stick to the letter of the law.

Make sure they know the rules from day one, remind them of the rules if they get off track, and enforce the rules & take action when necessary. I know this is simple advice, but this really is simple stuff.

Simple, but not easy. Simple means there is a system in place and a course of action ready to be implemented if the system begins to break down.

Try to be as proactive and levelheaded as possible, and your odds of being a successful landlord go up dramatically. Be reactive and caustic, and your odds of creating a successful business will go down in flames.

BONUS #4 Where to Get the $MONEY$

Fighting to get my good credit back after filing for bankruptcy in 1995 wasn't as hard as you may think. Most people slump into a corner after financial catastrophe and just assume that no one will ever loan them money again. When I bought my first property in 1996 it was under my wife's name and using her credit to get the loan. When I purchased our next rental, I used a small local bank for the loan and insisted that I be put on the loan with my wife. And they agreed. Less than two years after filing bankruptcy I had a mortgage loan showing on my credit report. From that point forward I made sure that every payment, on any loan or credit card, was paid on time.

Once my credit was reestablished with this mortgage, other lenders saw me as an acceptable risk as I began buying more property. By the time our first son was born in 1998 and my wife stopped working, I had rebuilt my credit completely. The bankruptcy in 1995 would be on my credit for ten years and have a negative impact, but I didn't let it slow me down for a minute.

There are two main strategies for getting money to buy property. One strategy is for the buy & flip purchase where you don't plan on holding onto the property for very long. The other is the buy & hold purchase typically used for a long-term rental property.

Fast Money

When buying for a quick flip, you need access to fast money. This money is very easy to find, but it's never cheap. Expect to pay several points and interest ranging from 12 to 18%. Many people cringe at the thought of such a high rate & use it as yet another excuse not to be successful. If you're buying at the right price, the interest rate should be irrelevant. If the difference between paying 7% and 14% interest makes your profit potential to tight, then your paying too much for the property.

Using fast money should get you better deals, though. Sellers love no financing contingencies and are usually willing to negotiate a lower price when there's no conventional loan involved.

So where do you find this bountiful resource of unlimited money? I've never had to look further than 2 easy places- my newspaper and title companies.

My Sunday edition has a separate section for Money To Lend and Money Wanted. I see ads all the time for people who want money and people who have money to lend. If your paper doesn't have a specific section then put an ad in the real estate section where investment properties are advertised.

Baltimore- Need 75k loan secured by
1ˢᵗ mortg. on house appraised at 125k.
will pay 15% interest. Dave 410-441-5525

Think you'll get one or two calls. You better believe it! Be prepared with your numbers when they do call. These types of private lenders come in all shapes and sizes. Some are whales and some are little fish looking to loan money for the first time.

Don't get offended, but these people don't care about you. They won't have your best interests in mind. Their looking to make a profit without a lot of headache and if your numbers sound promising, they will bite.

The other great place to find private lenders is with almost any title company. Think about it. There are hundreds, if not thousands, of real estate transactions every day in most major cities. The one common denominator is always the title company or settlement attorney. They know who the players are. They know who's selling lots of houses, who's buying lots of houses and who's doing the loans for all these deals.

It wasn't until March of 1999 & I had 6 properties under my belt that I used my first private lender. How did I get his name? I was at settlement for my sixth purchase and had developed a friendly relationship with my settlement company. As we were wrapping up I mentioned how I had my eye on a 3 unit building but was having trouble closing the deal.

On most of my previous purchases the seller was willing to hold a substantial 2nd mortgage. This allowed me to easily get 1st mortgages from a traditional lender and buy the house with very little or no money out of pocket. But this owner had no equity and I didn't have a wad of cash to make a $20,000 down payment.

Hearing all of this, the owner of the title company gave me a name & number of a private lender used often by other buyers. I called, introduced myself and described the deal. The private lender sent someone to do a 'drive by' appraisal (not formal, just checking neighborhood & outside condition of the house). The next day he told me he would loan me $95,000 at 14% interest, interest only monthly payments with the loan due in one year (a 1 year balloon loan). Perfect. I had negotiated a purchase price of 95k so in one fell swoop I had all the money I needed to buy this great building. After receiving a credit for the rents and negotiating a $4,000 credit from the seller to help cover my closing costs (all I did was ask & he said 'Yes'!), I was able to buy this terrific 3 unit building using a grand total of $631 of my own money.

I always made my payments on time to this lender so that I would be in his good favor for future deals. And my next deal using him was a whopper! Less than a year later I bought a package of 8 multi-unit buildings using a combination of money from this lender and the seller holding small 2nd mortgages on each house. In April 2000, I borrowed a total of $505,000 from this guy; someone I had never personally met. Someone who I wouldn't know if I was standing right next to him in a line. He never asked to see my credit. He couldn't care less about me.

The numbers looked good so he loaned the money. Most people don't believe this story when I first tell them, but I assure you it is 100% true!

Remember the Golden Rule:
Those with the gold get to make the rules.

That big settlement didn't go off perfectly. Between the private lender and the seller 2nd mortgages, I had 100% financing for each building. After factoring in the credit I would get at closing for all of the rents & security deposits, I was going to walk away from settlement with about $20,000 in my pocket.

This is when the rules changed. When I arrived at settlement I was informed that the private lender sent loan documents charging me 4 points (4% of the loan). He had not done this on the 95k loan so I never bothered to ask whether or not he charged points. I suspect that he saw the settlement sheets & noticed that I was going to leave with a large check and maneuvered at the last minute to keep that from happening. Notice that 4% of $505,000 is- $20,000! How convenient.

I either had to accept his terms or there was no deal. Without much fuss I bought the properties that day and although I didn't walk away with that big check, I only had to use $1,000 of my own money to buy 8 apartment buildings.

On another recent occasion, I was closing on a bank REO and mentioned to the settlement attorney (at a different title company) that I was trying to move quickly on a small deal. I needed $19,000 to buy a house that I could flip within a few months for $30,000. With the exception of cleaning it out, I wasn't planning on doing any major work. Someone else would buy it from me for 30k, make 15k in repairs, and rent it or resell it for profit.

Without even asking for it, the attorney offered to loan me the $19,000. He said he and his partner loan money all the time & that it was 'no big deal'. Amazing. I think that's when I really woke up & realized that the money was right in front of me all along; I just wasn't asking the right questions.

Start contacting title companies and ask them if they know of any private lenders. Do it before you even have any deals in the works just to prove to yourself that the money is out there. The hard part is finding a good deal on a house. Once you do, getting the money to buy it is simple.

To this day it boggles my mind that a lone, random individual loaned me half a million dollars and didn't know what I looked like. He never asked for my credit report and he never inspected the inside of the properties. I was buying at a low price and the numbers worked. Money flows to good deals like flies to honey, and nothing is sweeter than the taste of OPM, other people's money, to make your dreams come true.

Slow Money

When buying a rental property for the long haul you obviously want to get a low interest rate on your loan. My two best strategies are small local banks and private lenders.

Private lenders? Yes, but only as a way to get my foot in the door. That 3 unit building I bought for 95k was refinanced a year later with a traditional lender at a low interest rate. Sure I made a year's worth of very high interest loan payments, but the building was worth 140k when I bought it and appraised at 150k when I did the refinance. Don't be a penny wise and a dollar stupid when it comes to interest rates.

As I've said before, if the interest rate makes or breaks the deal, then you don't have a good deal. Most traditional lenders will do a refinance on a new purchase once you've owned it for 12 months. You may find some that will do it after only 6 months, but 12 months is the standard.

The other option is to forgo private lenders and use a bank or traditional lender for the purchase. I prefer using local banks over nationally recognized mortgage companies. Your local bank with a few branches probably meets once a week to discuss new loans. They will look at your last two tax returns, your credit report and the deal your putting forth & give a quick thumbs up or down. Their paperwork, in fact their entire process, is much less than the big lenders.

Another advantage is that you can establish a relationship with your local bank. They'll see you on a regular basis & you'll develop a comfort level for each other. This is important. One day you're going to have a deal that doesn't quite fit their guidelines and/or their comfort zone. But you know what? Odds are they'll approve it because of the relationship you've worked to establish.

The only real downside to not using a private lender is that your local bank will want a 20% down payment. The private lenders typically don't care about any of that. So long as their interest is protected (Ex. Loaning you 65k on a house worth 100k) the private lender won't care what money you do or don't have in the deal.

The best way to get the down payment is from the seller in the form of a 2nd mortgage or as a credit at settlement from the seller. In the whirlwind real estate market from a few years ago this would've been laughable. It's now summer of 2007 and no one is laughing now. They're ready to make a deal.

Go back and reread this bonus section again. Title companies and settlement attorney's have access to all the money you'll ever need to buy real estate. And you know what? Their eager to help you- they make money by doing real estate settlements! They want you to make as many settlements with them as possible and they're hungry for business. Go get em'.

BONUS #5 IT'S ALL IN YOUR HEAD!

It would be almost criminal to write this entire book without discussing your greatest asset- your mind. Taking your thoughts & dreams and turning them into reality is not complicated. It's never easy, though. As a society we look up to people like Oprah, Bill Gates, Donald Trump, Warren Buffet, Tom Cruise, etc. While all of these people have talent & have made their own unique mark on the world, the one thing they have in common is a <u>trained and conditioned mind</u>.

It doesn't matter what type of self-help book you've read, audio program you've listened to, or seminar you've attended; the building block of your success, or failure, begins with your mind. Learn to develop & train it and you will eventually succeed. Ignore it and you do so at your own peril.

You could very well still succeed, but your long-term success & overall happiness will suffer. Extreme examples are Anna Nicole Smith, Kurt Cobain and Elvis Presley. All of these people had tremendous influence, millions of fans and a ton of money! They had all the success and fame anyone could ever dream of, and yet they were all dead before the age of 50. Why?

Despite enormous success, none of them learned to train their mind. They lived in constant reaction to the world around them and instead of harnessing the tremendous power of their brain they used drugs & alcohol to escape reality. It's really sad.

I've read hundreds of books on self-help, psychology and success related topics. Many of them benefited me in some form and I continue to read 2 to 4 books a month to make sure I continue to grow as a person. There is one person, though, that I would recommend above all others. He is a best selling author and speaker. His books & audio programs have sold millions of copies around the world and for good reason- it works!

His name is Anthony Robbins.

If you've read his books or listened to his audio programs then you have an idea of what I'm talking about. If you've heard of him but never actually studied his work, it's time you investigated it thoroughly.

And if you've never heard of him, then prepare yourself for a complete mind makeover. His strategies for conditioning your mind to help you realize your dreams are powerful and easy to understand.

I've never personally met Tony, but after purchasing his first tape program years ago, <u>Unlimited Power- A 30-Day Program for Unlimited Success</u>, I was completely blown away. His strategies for conditioning your mind are innovative and amazing. They helped me quit smoking 14 years ago and it was easy & painless. It's not will power and it's not a positive thinking approach to life. It's a way to train your mind, to condition it, so that you're moving towards your goals and succeeding at the game of life.

While moving to our current house in 2002, I was cleaning out the desk in my home office and came across a couple of hand written sheets of paper from 1998. It was my notes from his tape program along with a list of goals. One of my goals in 1998 was to own 100 rental apartments within one year. Did I accomplish it?

No. I didn't have 100 apartments within one year, but within three years I did! As I looked over the list I realized that I had accomplished over 80% of my 1998 goals. All of this just didn't *happen*. To this day I use Tony's simple & effective strategies for success.

Here's just a small taste…..

At its most basic level your brain operates on pain vs. pleasure. Anything that gives you pain you will avoid and anything that gives you pleasure you'll want to move towards. The key is to stack the deck in your favor. You must use pain & pleasure to your advantage, or pain & pleasure will take advantage of you.

Recently, after twenty years of smoking, my wife abruptly quit. She didn't try to wean herself off by smoking less & less each day until down to zero. She didn't use nicotine patches or chew nicotine laced gum. She hasn't gained weight (in fact, she looks fabulous with all of those toxins out of her system). She was a little irritable for the first few days, but that subsided. We both shake our heads at how she voluntarily subjected her body to a host of chemicals and poisons daily for the last twenty years because of a supposed addiction to nicotine.

So what changed? She didn't take any magic pills or exotic diet. She didn't use willpower.

What changed was what she *associated* to smoking. In the past, she smoked even though she knew intellectually that it was harmful. But the bad outweighed the good. The pleasure she associated to smoking was more powerful than the supposed pain of quitting. Until she made a decision, a commitment, to quit.

When she told me she was about to quit, I immediately got her to use one of Tony's strategies. I told her to make a *written* list of all the pleasure she would have by quitting and make a list of all the pain she would experience if she continued to smoke.

Her list gave her the carrot and the stick at the same time & it motivated her without using willpower. Having things on her list like, 'Not being alive to see my kids graduate high school or get married' created a tremendous amount of pain for her. It was compelling enough to turn the tables and for the first time in twenty years, she associated pain to smoking. That's all it took.

Interestingly, a few weeks after she quit she told me about a dream. In it she was walking and came upon a lit cigarette on the ground. She immediately squashed it under her heel and continued walking.

I asked her why she did that. Her reply was, 'It never occurred to me to pick it up and smoke it, because I don't smoke'.

She had done such a good job of reconditioning her mind that even her subconscious was on board! When you use the powers of pain and pleasure to condition your mind, you become unstoppable.

I'm so proud of her.

And I'm proud of you too. Don't let this end here. This is only the beginning of your journey. Keep reading other books- at least two per month.

I highly recommend contacting AnthonyRobbins.com and discovering a wealth of tools that will help you grow & thrive. Always continue to feed your mind with new ideas and thoughts. The rewards are plentiful and well worth it.

To Your Success,

Dave Lawn

Sample Direct Mail Letter:

Dear Sir / Madam:

Do you:

- Own any vacant property?
- Own any property that needs work?
- Own a rental property that you're tired of dealing with?

Would you like to sell your property and receive **cash at settlement** and avoid a costly Realtor's commission?

My name is Dave Lawn and I have been purchasing real estate in Maryland since 1996. I will pay **cash** for any vacant or rental property that you own!

If you have an interest in selling a property, then please call me at 410-123-4567. All conversations are kept confidential.

I look forward to hearing from you soon.

Sincerely,

Dave Lawn

www.ingramcontent.com/pod-product-compliance
Lightning Source LLC
Chambersburg PA
CBHW051522170526
45165CB00002B/574